A man from Mars landed on Second Avenue in New York and looked into a store window, fascinated. Finally, he entered the shop and asked the owner: "What are those little wheels in the window?"

"Wheels? What wheels?"

The Martian pointed.

"Those aren't wheels," smiled the owner.
"They're called bagels. We eat them ... Here, try one."

The martian bit into a bagel and smacked his lips.
"Man! This would go great with cream cheese and lox!"

Eric Friedler/Peter Loewy

Bagels

Kehayoff

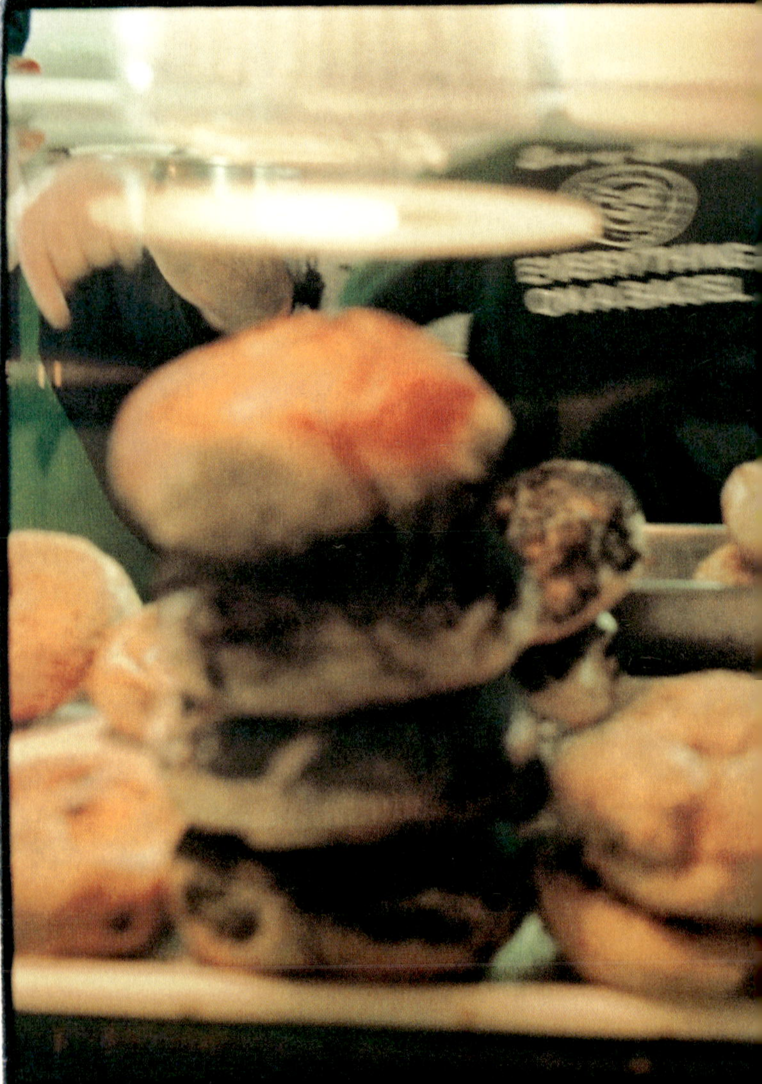

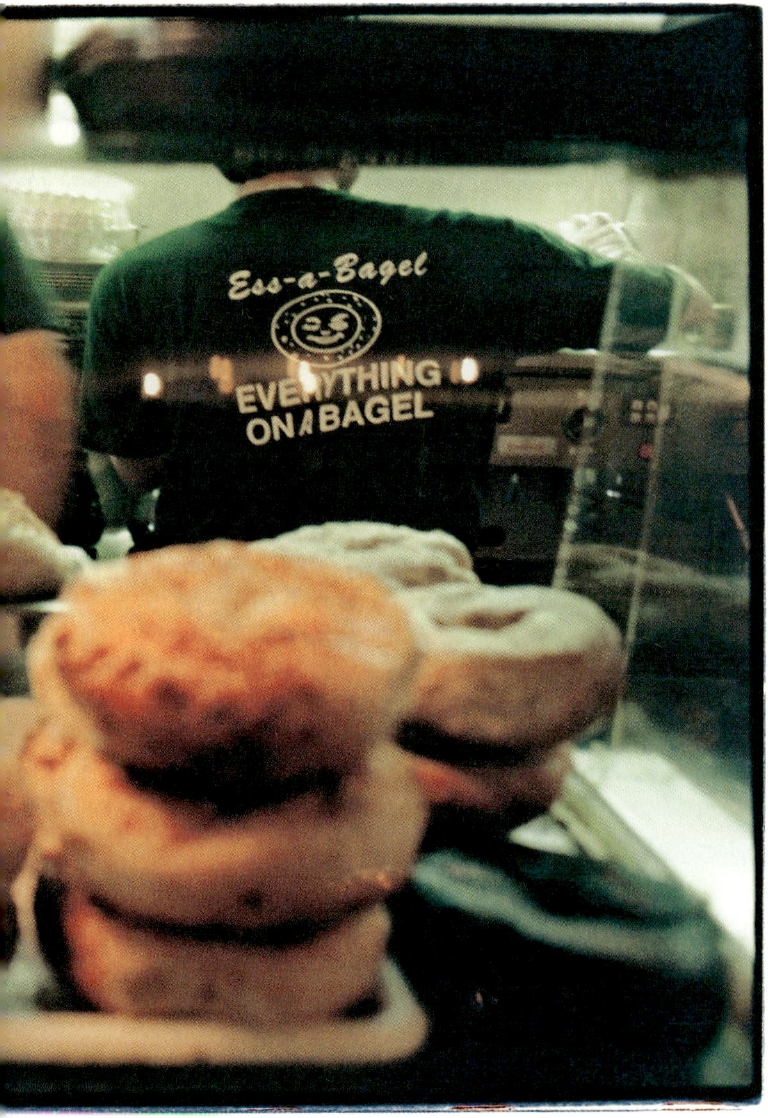

Ess-a-Bagel
EVERYTHING ON A BAGEL

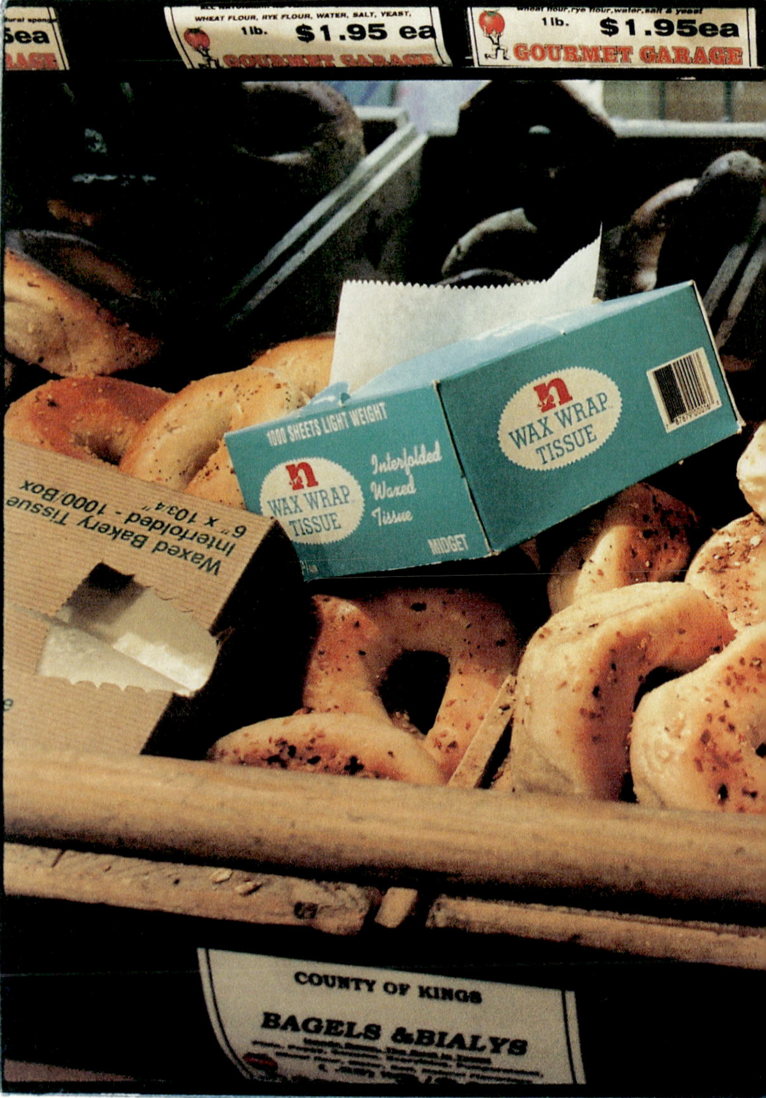
WHEAT FLOUR, RYE FLOUR, WATER, SALT, YEAST.
1lb. $1.95 ea
GOURMET GARAGE
wheat flour,rye flour,water,salt & yeast
1lb. $1.95ea
GOURMET GARAGE
1000 SHEETS LIGHT WEIGHT
WAX WRAP TISSUE
Interfolded Waxed Tissue
MIDGET
WAX WRAP TISSUE
Waxed Bakery Tissue
Interfolded - 1000/Box
6" x 10 3/4"
COUNTY OF KINGS
BAGELS &BIALYS

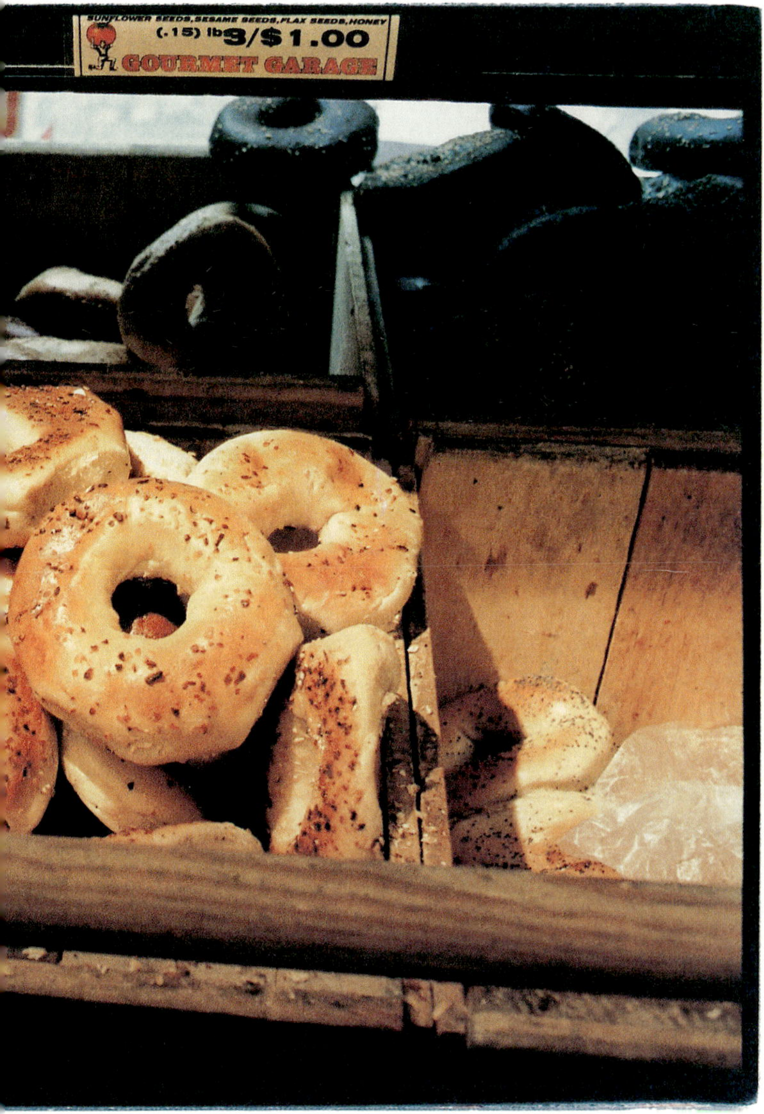

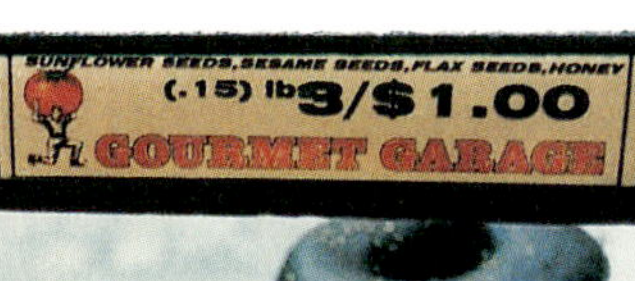
SUNFLOWER SEEDS,SESAME SEEDS,FLAX SEEDS,HONEY
(.15) lb 3/$1.00
GOURMET GARAGE

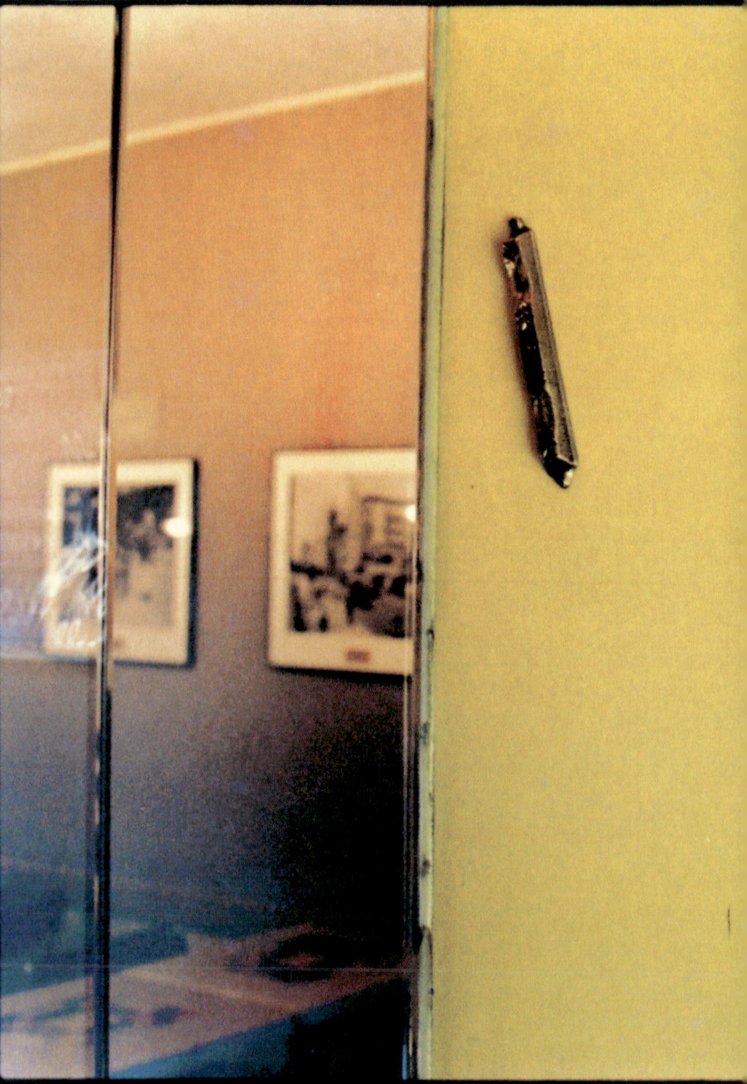

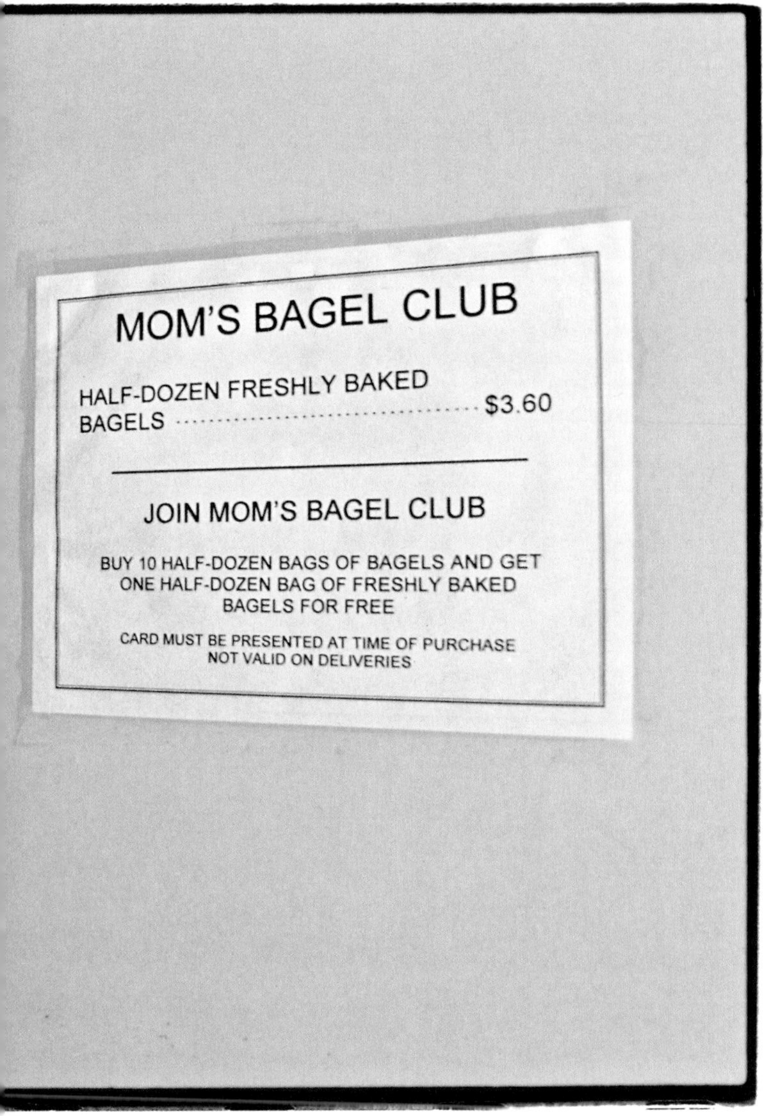

MOM'S BAGEL CLUB

HALF-DOZEN FRESHLY BAKED BAGELS $3.60

JOIN MOM'S BAGEL CLUB

BUY 10 HALF-DOZEN BAGS OF BAGELS AND GET ONE HALF-DOZEN BAG OF FRESHLY BAKED BAGELS FOR FREE

CARD MUST BE PRESENTED AT TIME OF PURCHASE
NOT VALID ON DELIVERIES

Rabbi Harry Cohen
165 WEST 91ST STREET
NEW YORK, N.Y. 10024
TEL. (212) 724-8663

December 31, 1996

KASHRUTH CERTIFICATION

To whom it may concern:

This is to inform you that the following establishment

KOSSAR'S
BIALYSTROKER KUCHEN BAKERY, INC.
367 GRAND STREET
NEW YORK, NEW YORK 10002

is under my strict Rabbinical supervision.

הרב דוד צבי הכהן
ניו יארק, נ. י.
RABBI H. COHEN

Harry Cohen
RABBI HARRY COHEN

Certification expires December 31, 1997

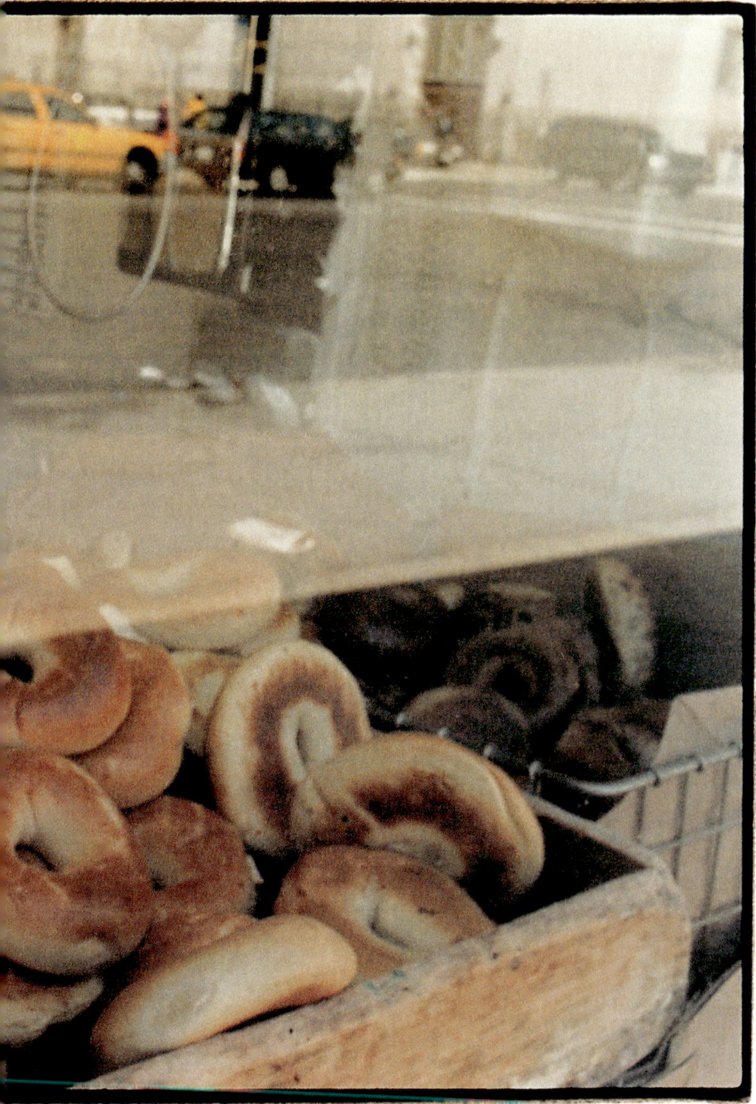

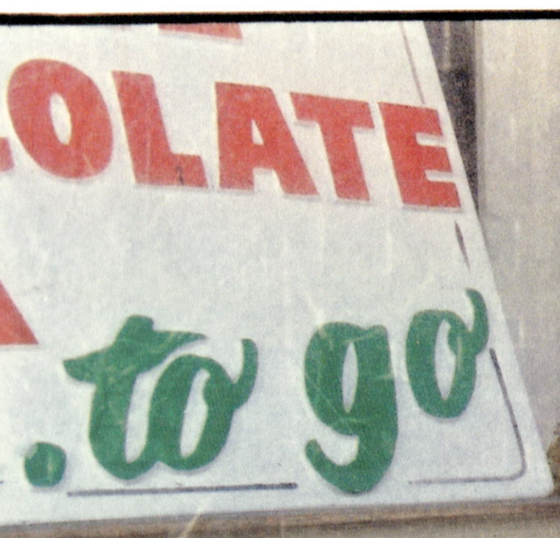
COLATE
to go

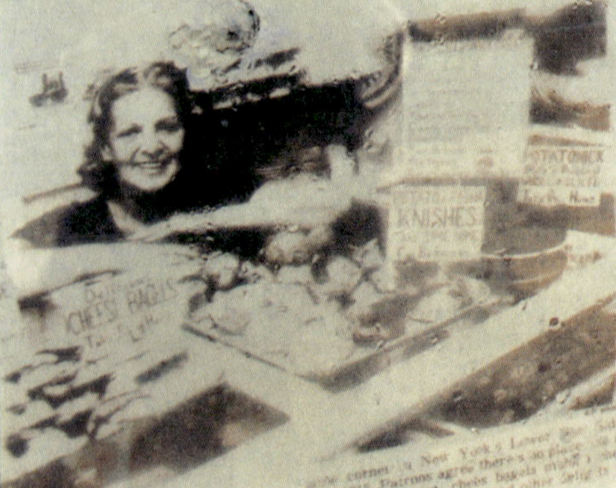
ew York Times
THURSDAY, JULY 23,
KNISHES

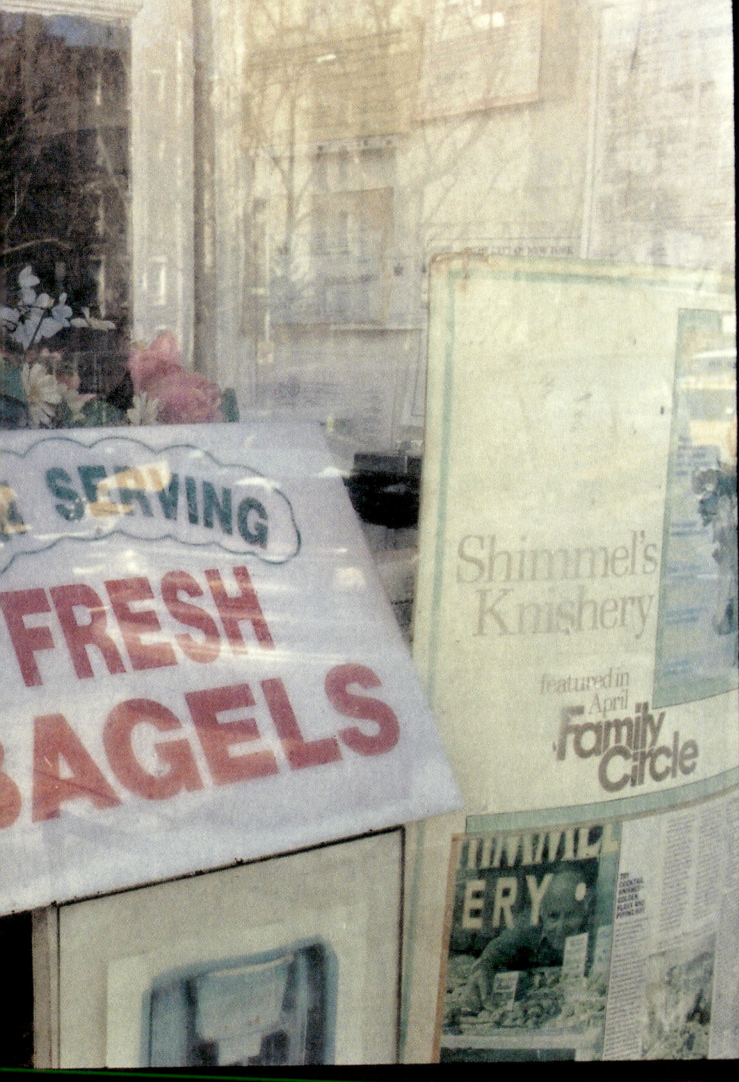
SERVING
FRESH
BAGELS
Shimmel's
Knishery
featured in
April
Family
Circle
ERY

In the beginning was the ring

A historical and literary overview of the bagel

Bagels are the perfect shape – an unbroken circle. This raises them above the level of mere nutrition, they are a metaphor for the cycle of life, for never-ending growth and decay. To eat a bagel was a symbolic act, not only at weddings and births, but also at funerals. A Yiddish folk song from Russia makes clear that bagels were also held to possess matchmaking qualities. Roughly translated, the song goes something like this:

"Let's go and buy some bagels
and spread butter on them
then Father and Mother will soon
lead you under the wedding canopy."

That was what they sang in the 19th century. The roots of the bagel can be traced back even further into the past, but its origins have been lost in the mists of time. But that is hardly surprising in the case of a bread whose form knows no beginning or end.

In all probability the bagel was simply just always there. In spite of this there have been various attempts to shed light on the origins of this mythical ring. One such theory is that the bagel was invented in Vienna in 1683. A Jewish baker is supposed to have created the bagel as a personal thank-you to the Polish King John III Sobieski (1629–1696). On 12 September 1683 King John and his army had routed the Turks in the battle of the Kahlenberg and relieved the siege of Vienna. The bagel – according to this theory – is actually a representation of a stirrup (German: "Buegel"), for the King of Poland was a passionate rider. Thus the Viennese baker formed the first bagel in praise of King John, the great horseman and liberator.

This story sounds plausible; but if the bagel was invented in Vienna in 1683, how did it find its way onto the statute books of the city of Cracow in 1610? According to a decree of the city council of the time, the consumption of bagels became the exclusive right of women who had recently given birth and wet-nurses. In doing so they decreed that bagels were a source of nutrition reserved solely for women at a critical time of their lives. The reason for this strange edict is not known. Perhaps it is linked to the symbolic power and magical effects attributed to the bagel. These special powers were particularly said to strengthen women after child-birth. In any case one thing is certain: seventy years before the Turkish siege of Vienna the Cracow city councillors had already recognized that bagels were no ordinary sort of bread. However, the search for the original bagel by diligent historians, as this short historical overview shows, has still not been completed.

Crispy bagels were originally a typical form of sustenance for the Jewish population of Poland and Russia, but even in previous centuries they caught the attention of non-Jews. This fact is illustrated by an anecdote from the 18th century.

The famous Rabbi Israel Baal Shem Tov was trying to make clear to a simpleton how valuable a bagel was. The Rabbi convinced him that he should always carry one with him, for they possessed particular powers. If he should get into trouble, all he had to do was to throw it and then even Christians would come rushing to his aid. And indeed: one day the simpleton fell into a river and thought he was going to drown. There were two people on the bank of the river, but they didn't notice him. Suddenly he remembered the

Rabbi's advice and fished a soaking but, thanks to its special consistency, still intact bagel out of his trouser pocket and hurled it with all his strength towards the bank. This unusual projectile had the required effect and Jews and Gentiles rushed to drag him out of the water.

One of the best stories concerns the fools in the city of Chelm, who tried to get to the bottom of the secret of the bagel. Chelm is a fictional city that features in the stories of Eastern Europe, whose inhabitants are, of course, far more stupid that we could ever be.

In Chelm, the town of fools, the Town Council once sat for seven days and nights and finally resolved to send a delegation out into the wide world to see if there was something worth bringing back to Chelm. The delegation from Chelm wandered around the world for a long time and saw nothing they considered worthwhile introducing into Chelm, except for one thing they saw in Vilnius. Now, what was Vilnius famous for? For its fine bagels, of course. The Chelmans had never seen nor tasted anything like these delicious rings of crusty dough. After each delegate had eaten at least two dozen bagels, the senior member exclaimed, "I am an old man, but never in all my life have I tasted any food as delicious as this."

Then and there the delegation decided to learn how to make bagels and to bring the secret back to their home town. They went to the baker and promised to pay him any price if he agreed to teach them how to make bagels. The baker told them that there was nothing easier. "Take some round holes, put some dough around them, simmer them in a pot of boiling water, then pop them in the oven and out will come your bagels."

The Chelmans were still puzzled. "But where do we get the holes?" they asked. "First you buy the bagels from me," explained the baker, "then you eat them and use the holes again to make more bagels."

So all the delegates bought themselves strings of bagels which they hung round their necks. They paid the bagel baker for his lesson and happily set out for Chelm. On the way they came to a steep mountain slope, where the dean of the group exhorted them, "Fellow Chelmans, we must observe our tradition of not carrying anything down a slope which can roll down by itself."

So the members of the delegation took off their bagel necklaces and threw them off the top of the slope so that they could roll down by themselves.

Now at the foot of the hill there happened to be a pack of hungry dogs who smelled the bagels and began devouring them.

When the Chelmans came down the slope and saw what the dogs were doing, they began to shout, "Never mind the bagels, but please be careful with the holes! For heaven's sake, please don't touch the holes!"

But dogs will be dogs and as they wolfed down the bagels, they paid no attention to the holes. Alas, the Chelmans searched high and low, but couldn't find a single hole.

Mournful and downcast, the delegation trudged back to Chelm, with no bagels and no holes and because of this, there are no bagels in Chelm to this very day.

Several Yiddish sayings give some idea of the price of a bagel. For example: "When you eat a bagel, where does the hole go? – Into your pocket!" From this we can assume that bagels were not exactly cheap. Or perhaps it was simply that after eating the first you have to have a second and a third ... In this case the saying can be interpreted as a warning against an expensive addiction – a disease that still afflicts many bagel-eaters today!

Another saying goes: "It's like a bagel for a penny." This suggests that the price of bagels was probably always a fixed constant, in contrast to the price of other groceries where it was possible to haggle.

People laughed at sayings and stories like these in market squares all over Eastern Europe, where bagels were on sale for everybody. In Russia they were known, incidentally, as "bublitchki"; in the Forties the Barry Sisters, the Yiddish-singing soul singers, sang about them under the same name. They called their song "Bublitchkee baygelakh":

Buhblichkee baygelakh,
haysinkeh baygelakh, du koyft.

Es kimt balt oon dee nakht,
ikh shtay sikh teef fahrtrakht,
zahyt mahyne aygehlakh
zehnen fahrshmakht.

Der frost in droysen brent,
fahrfroyren mahyneh hent,
fin tsuress zing ikh mir mahyn troyrik leed,
nu koyfche buhblichkee, haysinke baygelakh
dee letsteh baygelakh nu koyft bahy meer!

Ikh shtee alayn in gahss
fin raygen ver ikh nahss,
dee letsteh baygelakh du koyft bahy meer!

Dee nakht es gayt fahrbahy,
der tog kimt oon afs nahy,
ikh shtay in gahss in trakht, vos vet du zahyn.

Der waytik iz zehr groys,
fin hinger gay ikh oys,
du menchen hehrt mahyn leed
fin hingerpahyn.

Buhblichkee, baygelakh,
koyft mahyneh buhblichkee, koyft!

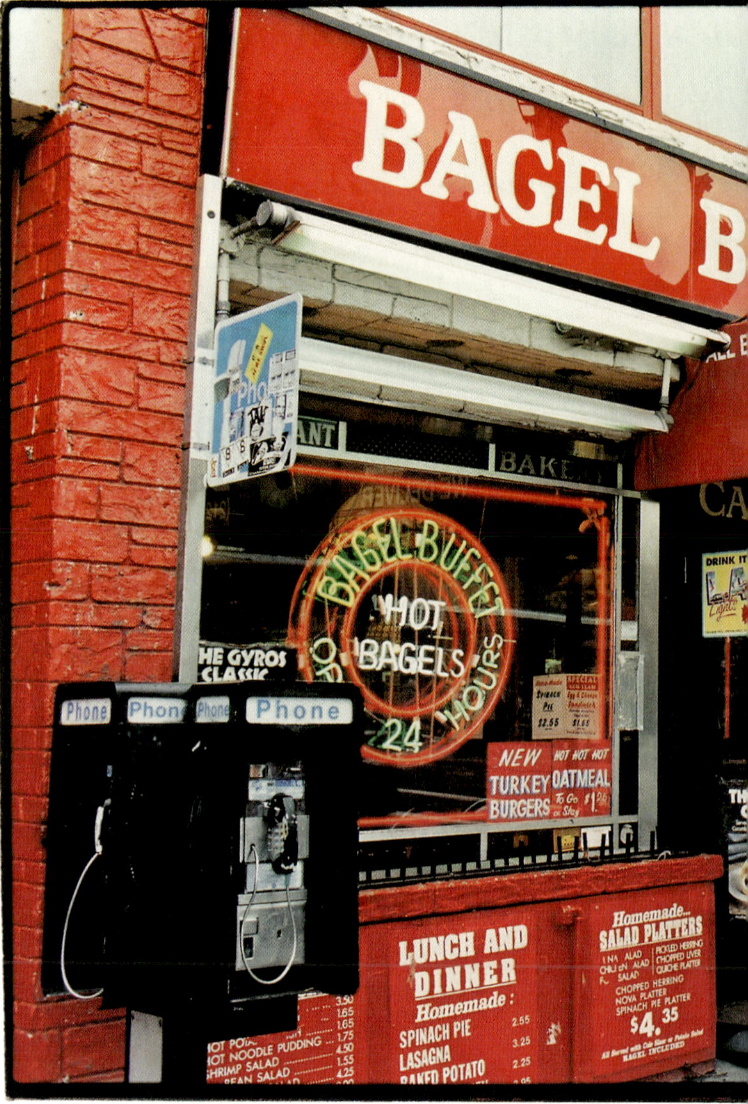
BAGEL
BAKE
BAGEL BUFFET
HOT BAGELS
24 HOURS
Phone
Phone
Phone
Phone
NEW TURKEY BURGERS
HOT HOT HOT OATMEAL
DRINK IT
LUNCH AND DINNER
Homemade :
SPINACH PIE 2.55
LASAGNA 3.25
Homemade...
SALAD PLATTERS
PICKLED HERRING
CHOPPED LIVER
QUICHE PLATTER
CHOPPED HERRING
NOVA PLATTER
SPINACH PIE PLATTER
$4.35
HOT NOODLE PUDDING ... 4.50
SHRIMP SALAD ... 1.55

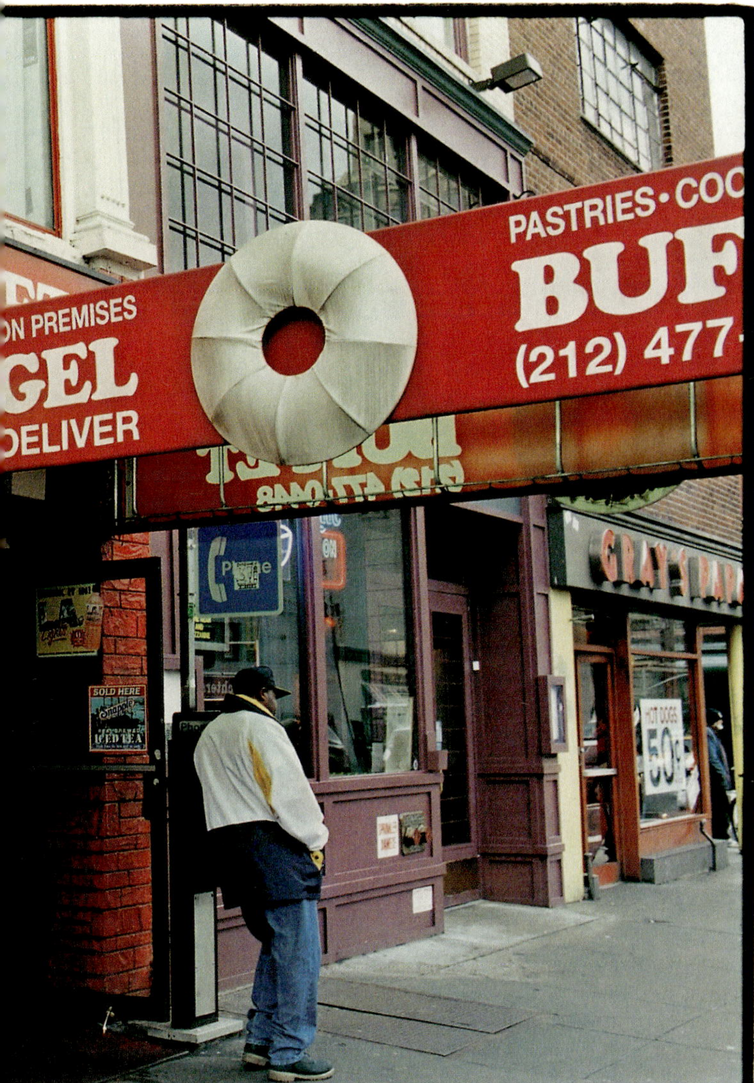
ON PREMISES
GEL
DELIVER
PASTRIES · COO
BUF
(212) 477-
Phone
SOLD HERE
Snapple
ICED TEA
HOT DOGS
50¢
GRAY'S PAP

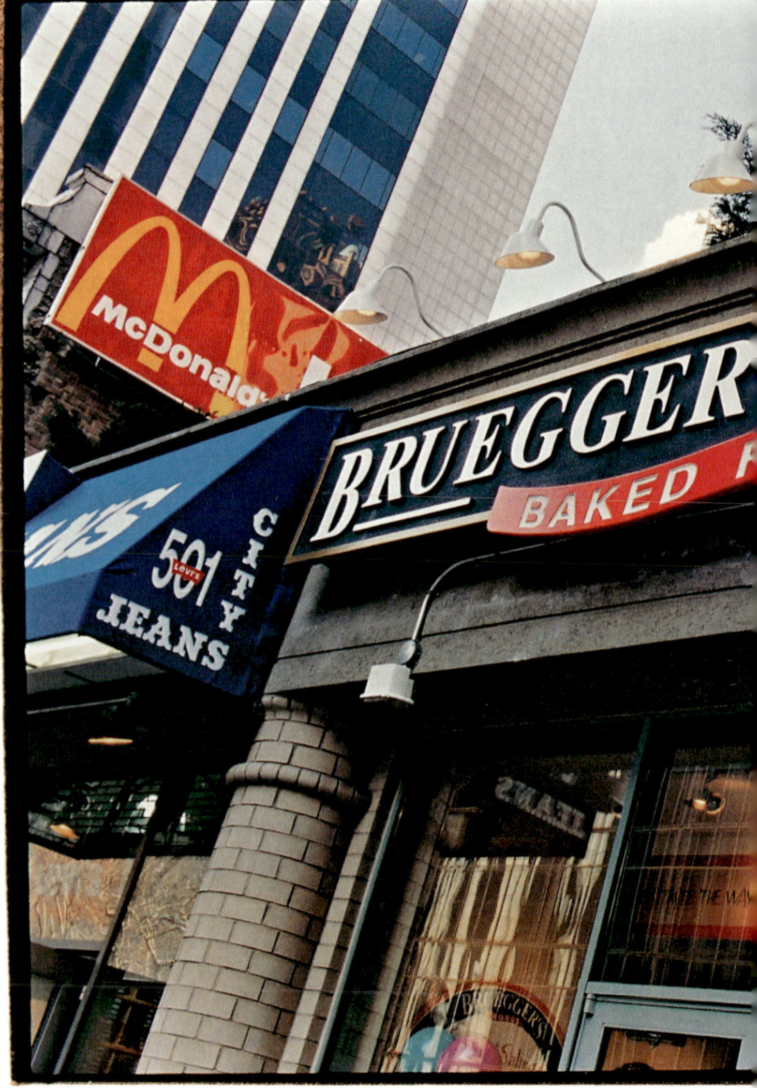
McDonald
BRUEGGER
BAKED
501
CITY
JEANS

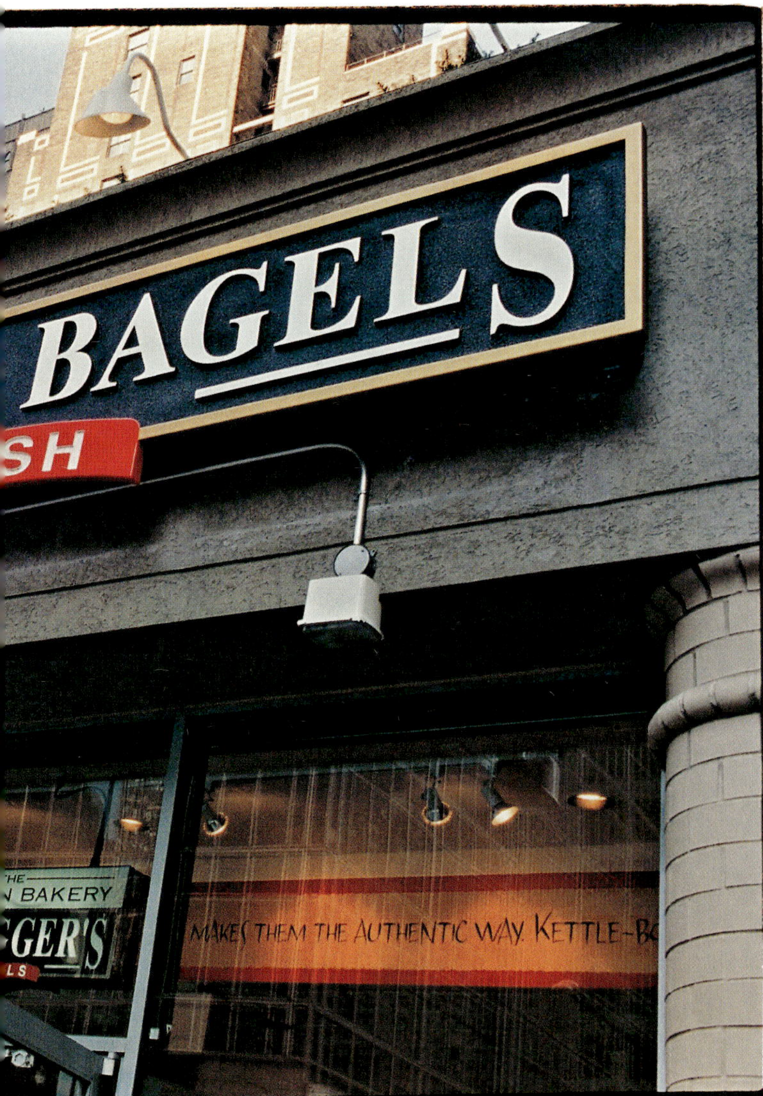
BAGELS
MAKES THEM THE AUTHENTIC WAY.

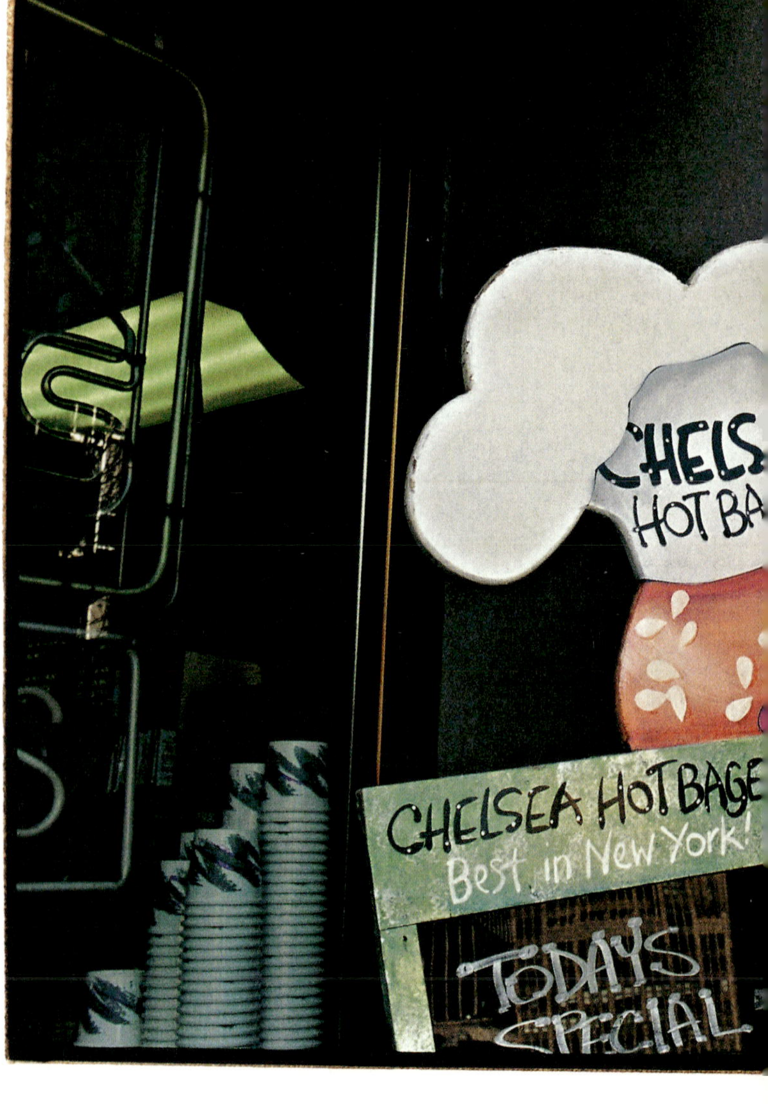
CHELS
HOT BA
CHELSEA HOT BAGE
Best in New York!
TODAYS
SPECIAL

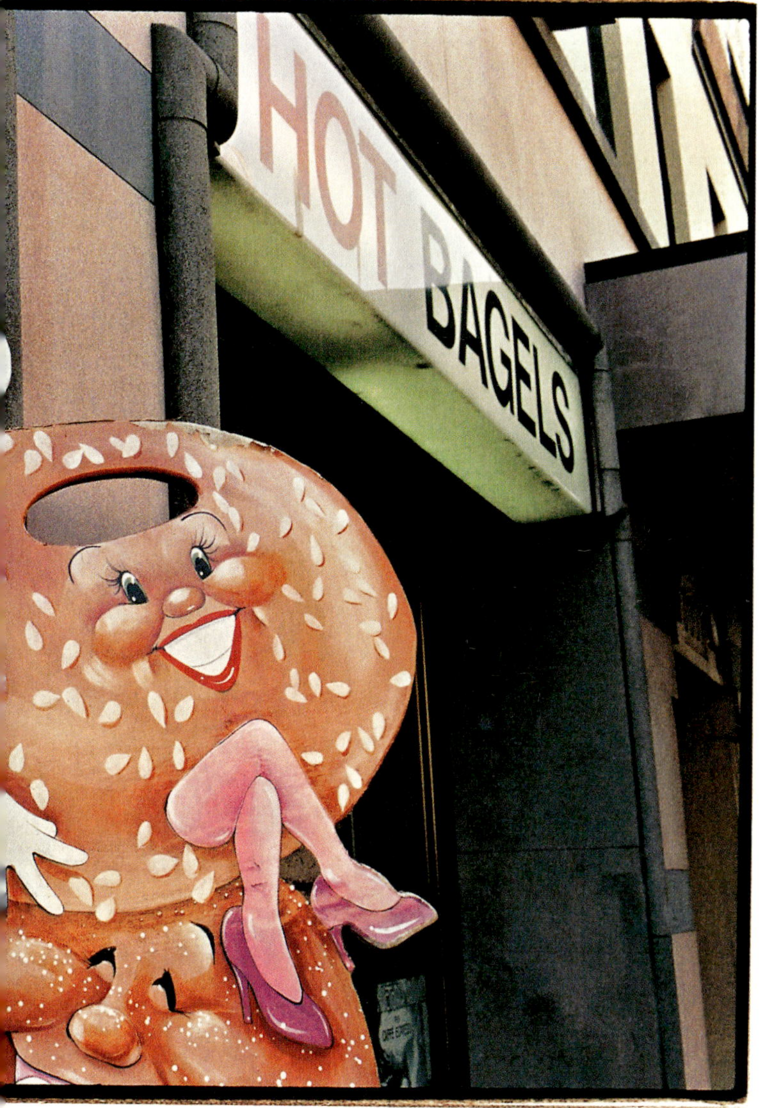
HOT BAGELS

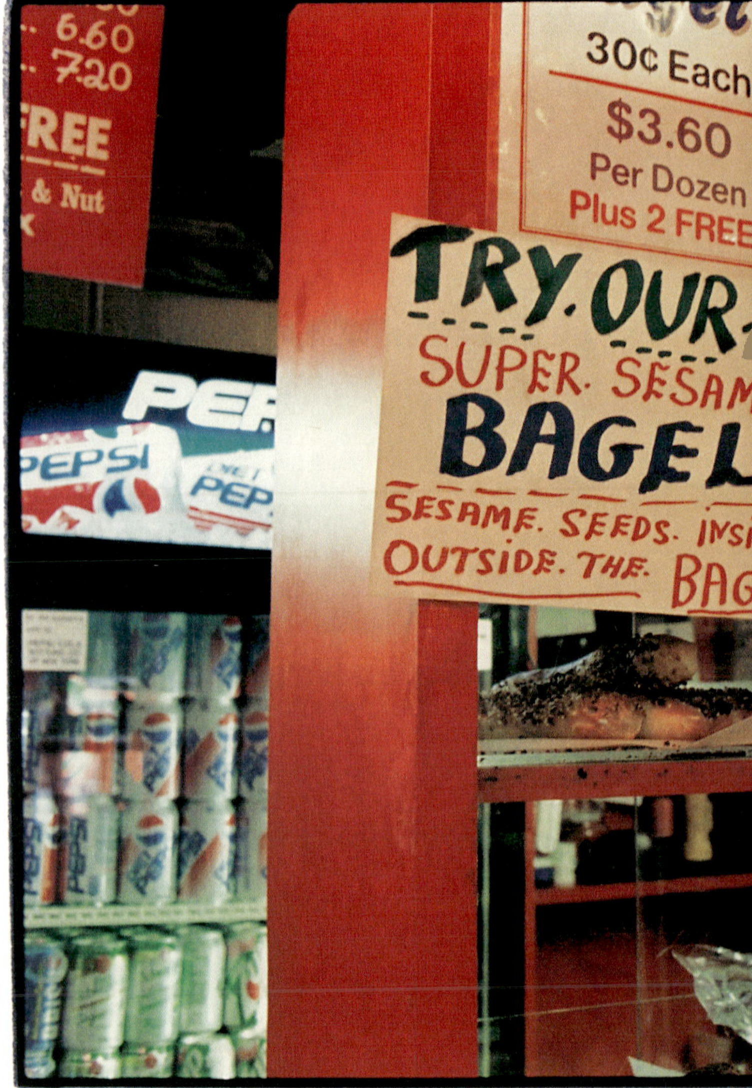
6.60
7.20
& Nut
30¢ Each
$3.60
Per Dozen
Plus 2 FREE
TRY. OUR.
SUPER. SESAM
BAGEL
SESAME. SEEDS. INSI
OUTSIDE. THE. BAG
PEPSI

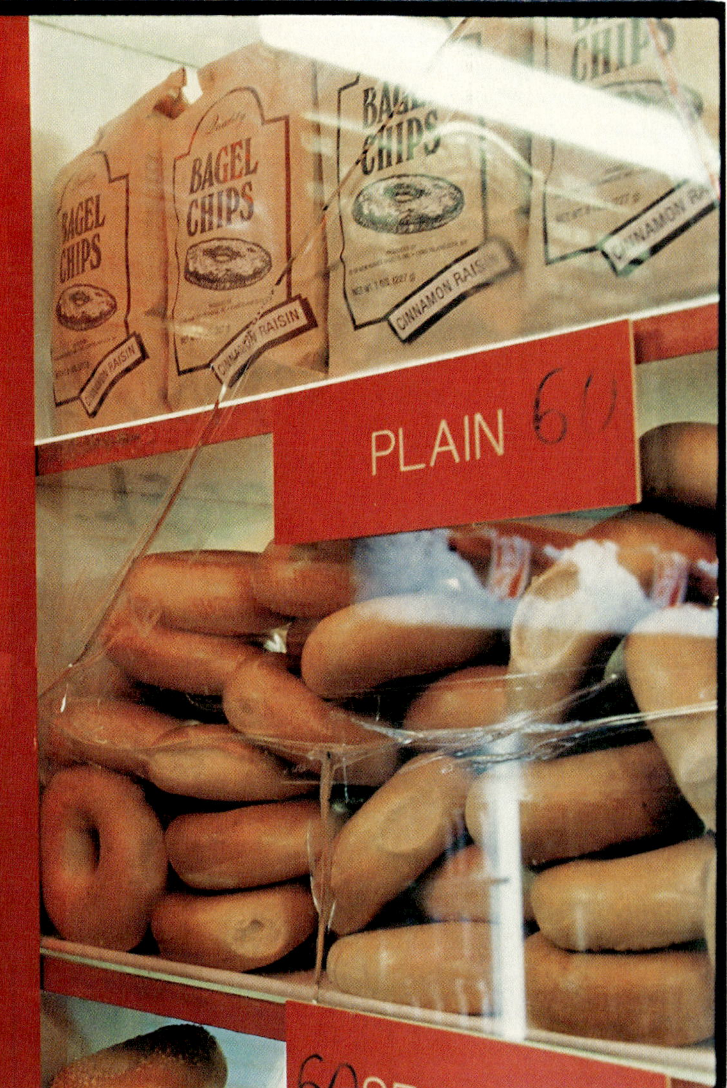
BAGEL CHIPS
CINNAMON RAISIN
BAGEL CHIPS
CINNAMON RAISIN
BAGEL CHIPS
CINNAMON RAISIN
PLAIN 60

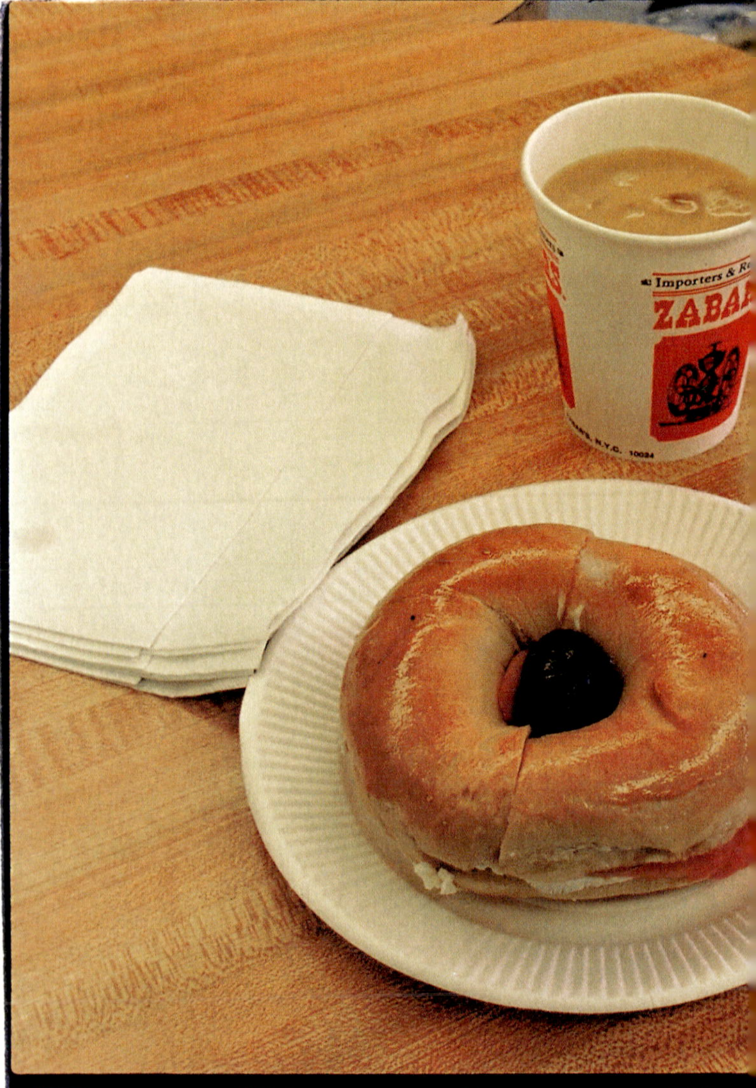
Importers &
N.Y.C. 10024

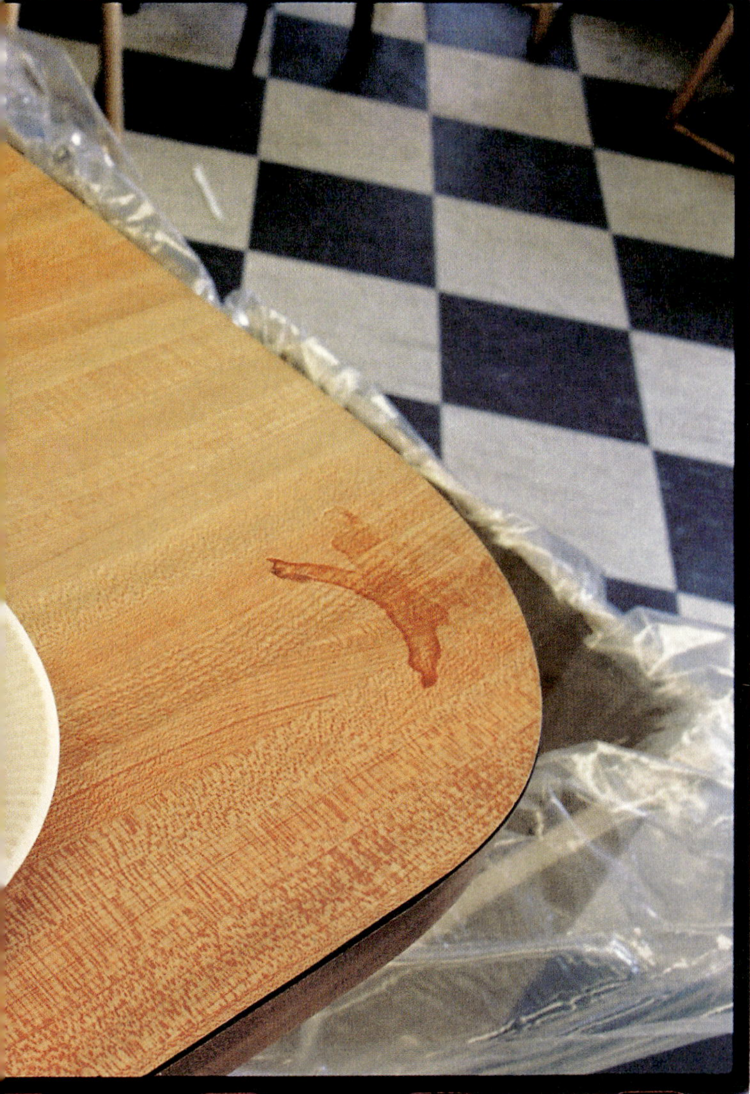

From the basement to the first floor
The inexorable rise of the poor bread ring

The historical excursion has shown that bagels were popular and sought-after in the Old World. But the bagel's career only really began when it left its roots behind and set sail for the New World.

At the start of the 20th century thousands of poverty-stricken Eastern European Jews emigrated to the United States. They set off with empty pockets and big dreams of happiness, wealth and freedom. Bagels also played a part in these dreams, as a late 19th-century Yiddish folksong from Lithuania shows:

> *"I am the bridegroom, you are the bride,*
> *We are both equal.*
> *In America we can bake bagels,*
> *Enough bagels for a whole year."*

For people who only lived from hand to mouth, "enough bagels for a whole year" was a symbol of wealth and luxury!

The Jewish immigrants first settled in the poor Lower East Side of New York. They brought their eating habits as well as their dreams with them and so the first bagel bakeries in America sprang up in this neighbourhood. Bagels were a piece of "home" that even abroad didn't lose any of their attraction. Moreover, as an economical, tasty and nutritious food they were just the right thing for hard-working people who had to think twice about every penny they spent. Culinary refinements such as salmon and cream cheese still lay in the future. At the turn of the century bagels were mostly eaten on their own, sometimes with butter or as a filling side-order to simple dishes.

People who ate bagels in those days were poor and the ambiente in the places where bagels were baked was correspondingly unappetizing. They were baked in basements, in gloomy and musty cellars, where night for night the brick ovens glowed. The bagel bakers worked in teams, each team consisting of four men. Two formed the bagels, one simmered them in a huge kettle of boiling water, and one shoved tray after tray into the oven. The finished bagels were packed in boxes, each containing 64 bagels. The men were paid 19 cents a box. In one night a skilled team of bakers could fill one hundred boxes. In spite of the proletarian surroundings it was possible even then to earn a lot of money with bagels.

It didn't take long until the bagel bakers decided to form a cartel to protect their market from competition. In 1915 three hundred members joined together and proclaimed self-confidently that they had "bagels in their blood", meaning that they were descendants of immigrant bagel bakers. They signed an agreement that they would only hand down their baking skills and recipes within the family dynasty, so as not to endanger the monopoly. The Union was an exclusive club – membership was passed on from father to son. At that time there were 36 so-called "Union Bagel Shops" in New York and New Jersey.

It was supposed to be harder to get an apprenticeship in one of these bakeries than it was to get a place at medical school – so they say. The Jewish mothers weren't very pleased, that their sons became bagel bakers. They dreamed, then as now, that their sons should become "a Doktor".

We shouldn't forget that there were also some people who were opposed to bagels. One example of this is the following item that appeared in the New York Times in May 1946. An incensed housewife from the Bronx apparently sent each of three Washington politicians a bagel and the following furious note: "This is what bread will look like in the future if the Government doesn't do something soon to stop bakers reducing the size of a standard loaf of bread. All that will be left is a hole with a bit of dough around it!" This didn't seem to halt the growth of the bagel industry, however.

The "holes with a bit of dough around them" were made by hand up until the Sixties. This remained unchanged until the Canadian Dan Thompson invented a bagel baking machine, finally fulfilling the dream of his father, a bagel baker from Winnipeg. Mr Thompson senior had been brooding over the plans of a machine to make the tough manual work redundant since 1926. And he wasn't the only one obsessed by the idea. During the Twenties there were more than fifty attempts to invent such a machine. But none of them were successful – compared to the skillful teams of bakers the machines were still too slow and expensive. Dan Thompson achieved the breakthrough, however. His "Thompson Bagel Machine Company" developed the first commercially-successful model. It took a while for the machine to establish itself, but in the large cities on the East Coast the ever-increasing hunger for bagels could no longer be satisfied by non-mechanical means. At first the bakers rented the machines, but business was booming and soon even small family bakeries were able to afford one of the Thompson Company's models. One machine could produce 2100 bagels an hour – the teams of bakers couldn't compete any longer.

This also brought about changes in the bakeries. In 1963 the New York Times reported that all twenty-six bagel shops in Manhatten were now residing on the first floor. Clean shops, with neon lights flashing at the front, advertising "hot bagels". Gleaming stainless steel ovens signalled to the ever-welcome customers: cleanliness is our goal. This was, incidentally, registered with particular satisfaction by the Board of Health because the subterranean bakeries were breeding grounds for dangerous germ. For their owners, the descendants of the Jewish immigrants who had once slaved away in the basements of the Lower East Side, these shops were the fulfillment of their American Dream. For them bagels were no longer a part of their past in the ghettos of Eastern Europe, they were a symbol of a golden future in the land of opportunity.

The bagel became Americanized. Just how much so is shown by the following incident from the Cold War era. In 1962 employees of a large bagel bakery on Long Island demonstrated their patriotic feelings under the slogan: "American onions are OK; keep out communist onions". They steadfastly refused to flavour their bagels using Bulgarian onions. Their boss tried to force them to knead the "communist onions" into their bagel dough, but their threat of strike action was successful – the owner of the bagel bakery was forced to give in and replaced the "red" Bulgarian onions with home-grown American ones.

Since the Sixties the golden ring has stood alongside Coca-Cola and the other American achievements. The era of the musty basement vaults was finally over – the inexorable career of the bagel from street urchin to the star of the bakery had begun.

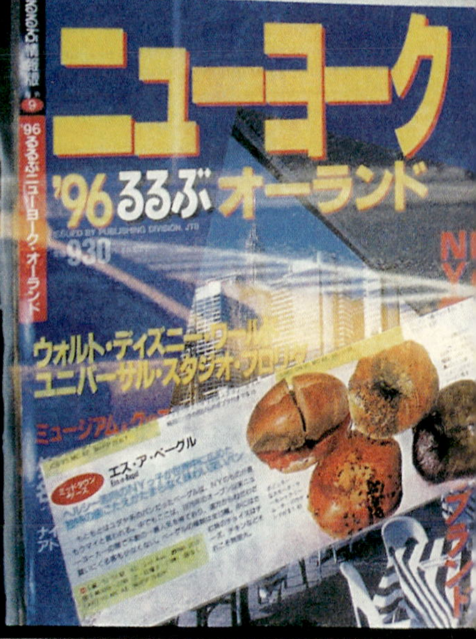
ニューヨーク
'96るるぶ オーランド
'96るるぶニューヨーク・オーランド
930
エス・ア・ベーグル

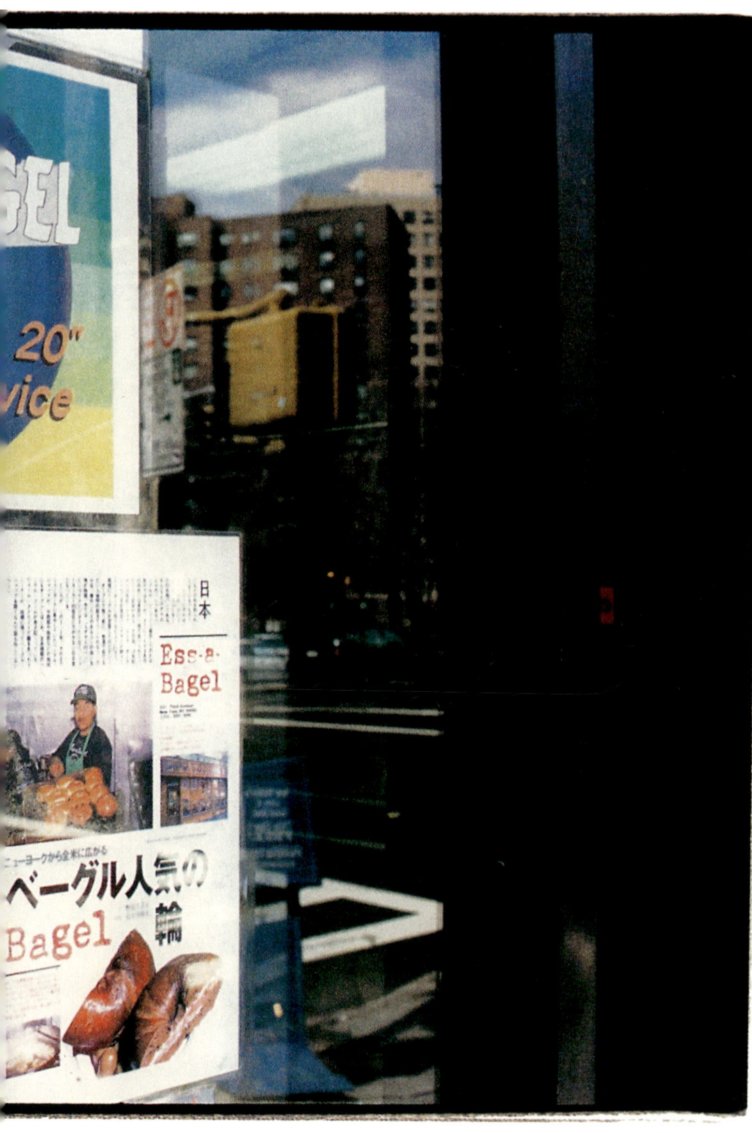
GEL
20"
vice
日本
Ess-a-
Bagel
ニューヨークから全米に広がる
ベーグル人気の
輪
Bagel

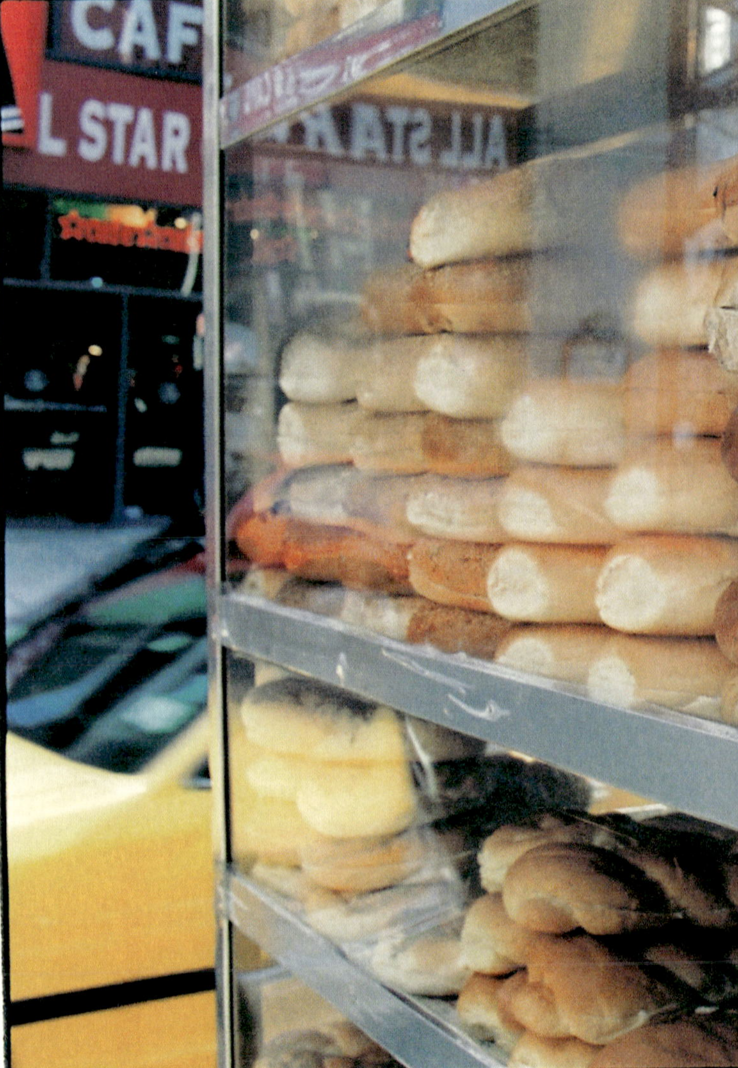
CAF
L STAR

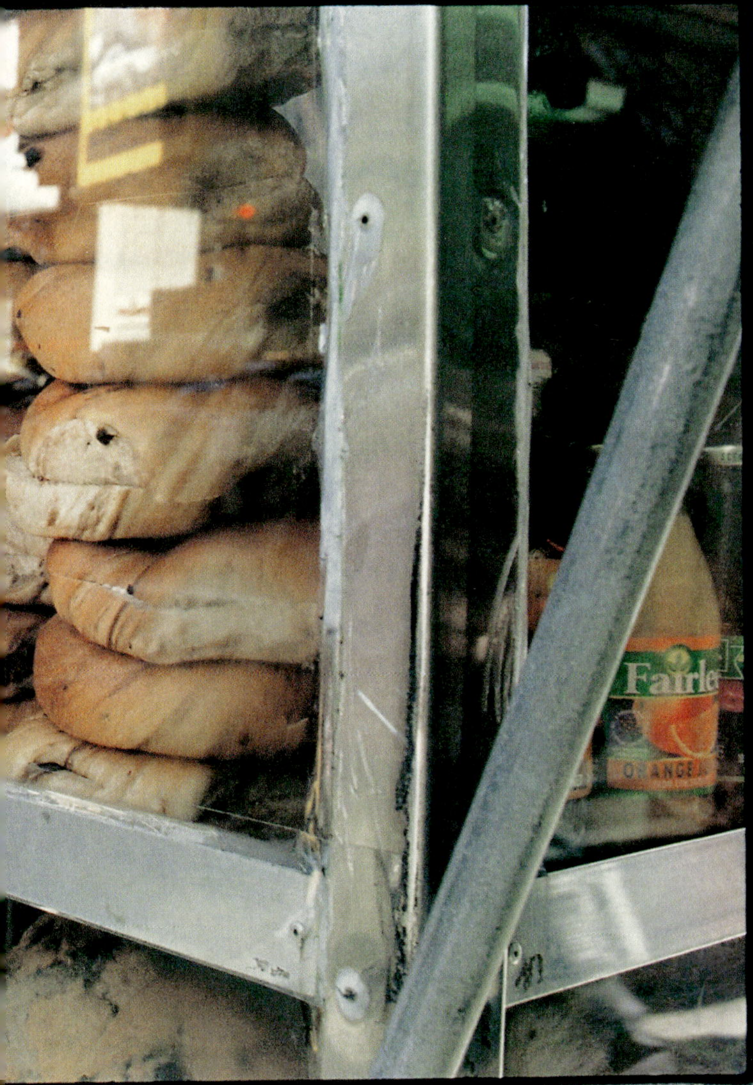
Fairle
ORANGE

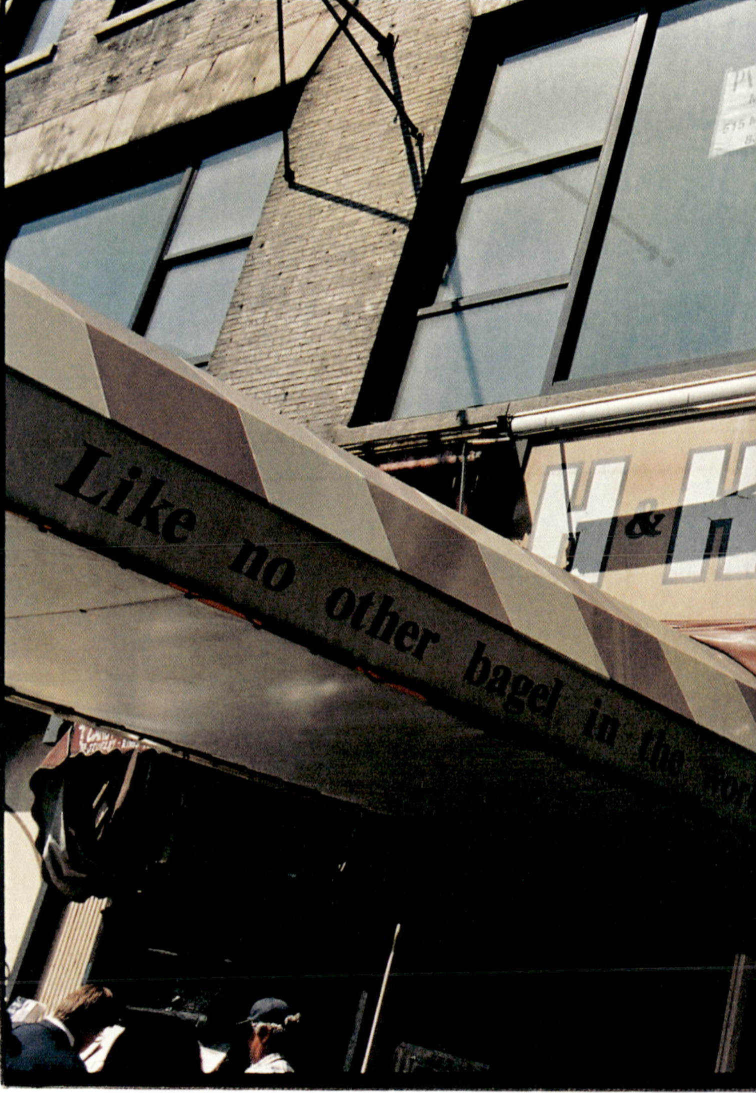
Like no other bagel in the

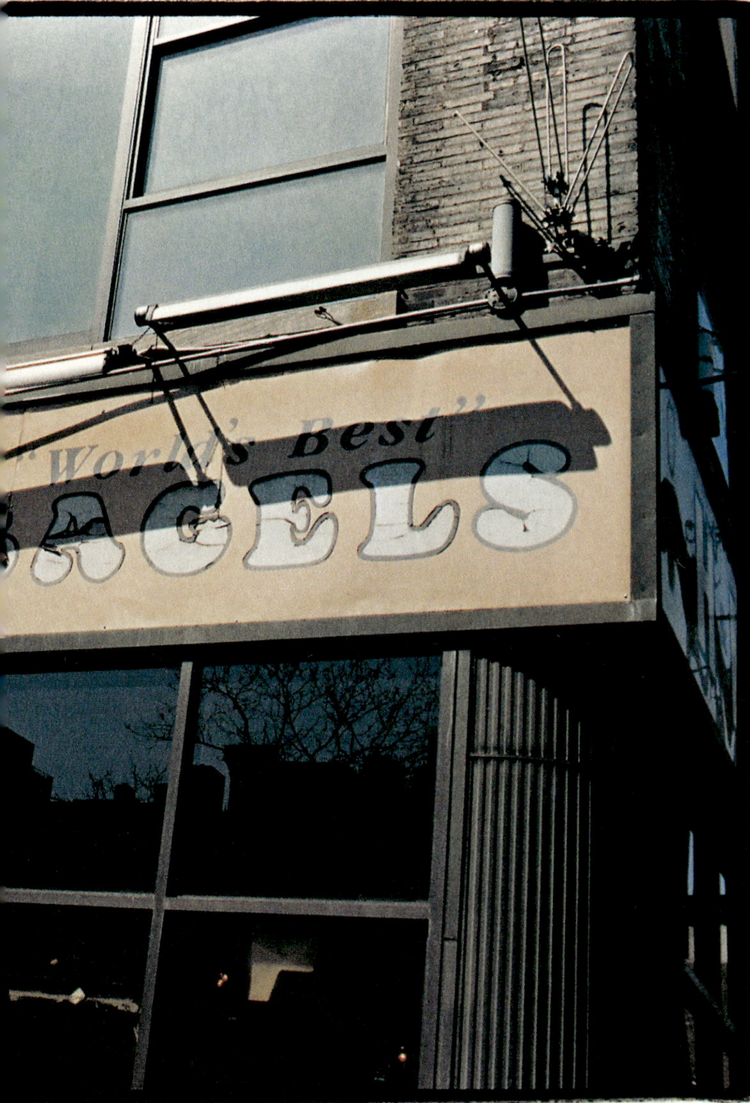
"World's Best"
AGELS

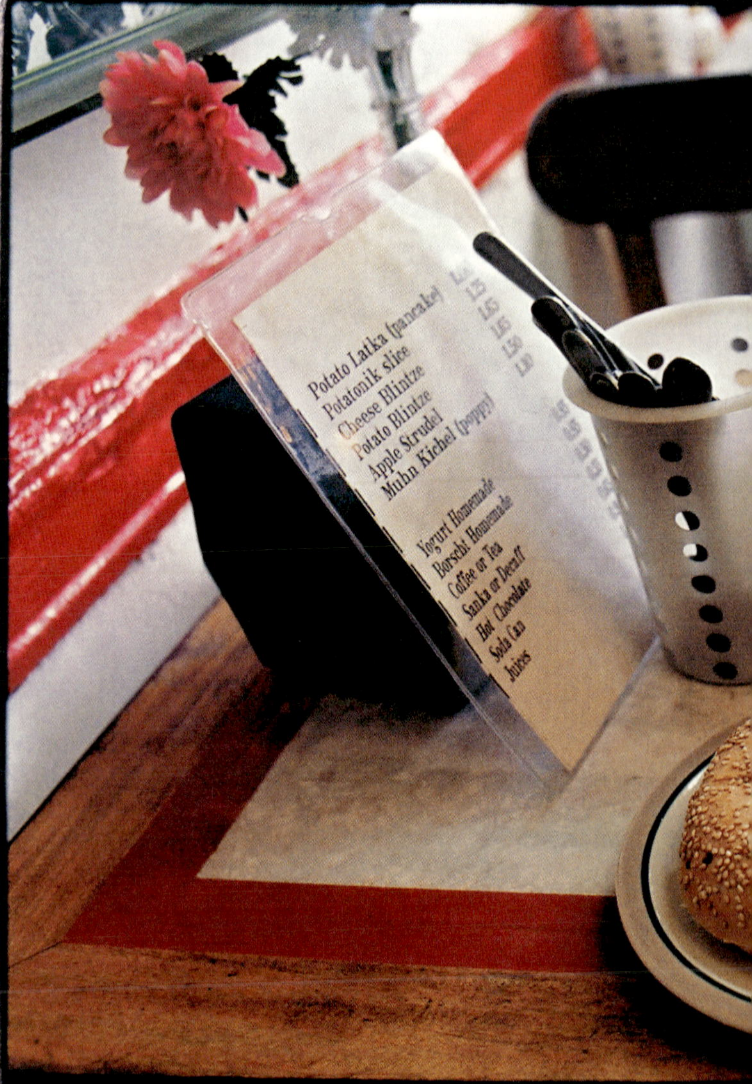
Potato Latka (pancake)
Potatonik slice
Cheese Blintze
Potato Blintze
Apple Strudel
Muhn Kichel (poppy)
Yogurt Homemade
Borscht Homemade
Coffee or Tea
Sanka or Decaff
Hot Chocolate
Soda Can
Juices

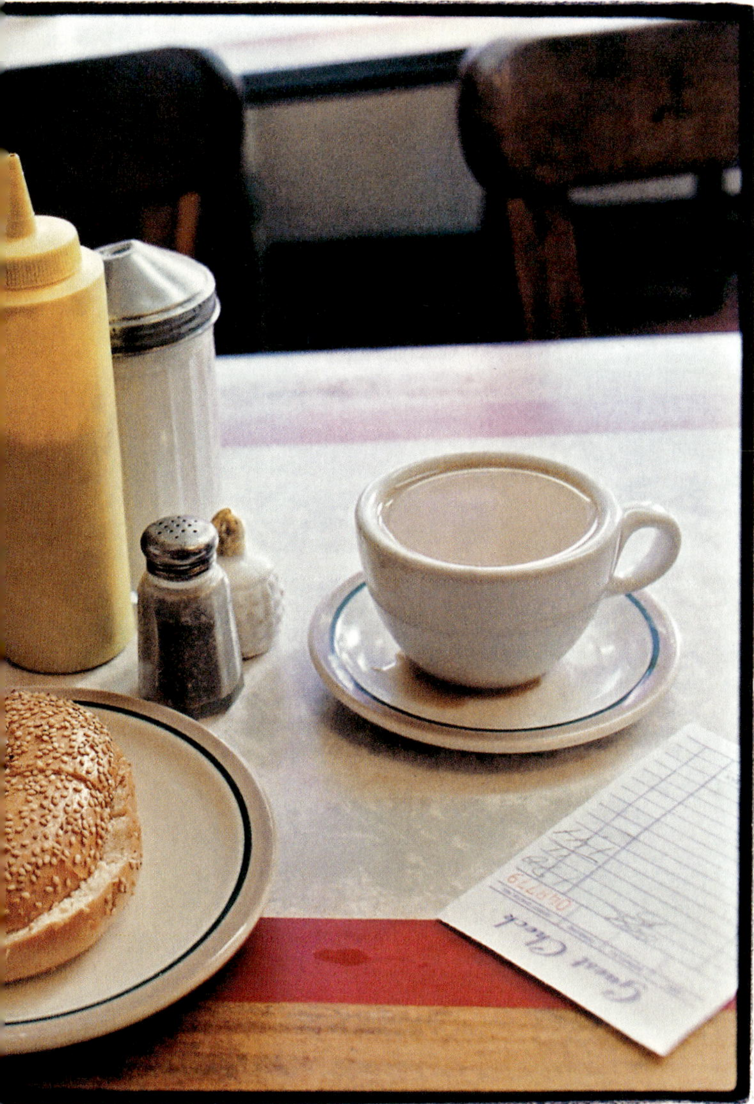
Guest Check

Bagels on everyone's lips

Until the Fifties bagels remained a typical bread of Jewish immigrants and their descendants. But just as the pizza has left its Italian roots far behind and has become a national dish, so the bagel has also conquered the hearts and stomachs of the nation. On the breakfast table, in coffee shops, restaurants, fast-food stores, gas stations, supermarkets and of course in the classic bagel shops – Americans are crazy about bagels and spend over a billion dollars a year on them.

In 1951 bagels first appeared in the headlines on the front page of the New York Times. According to the article, "New Yorkers frightened by threatened bagel shortage. The bagel bakers' strike is causing difficulties of supply." It went on to report that 300 bagel bakers were striking for higher wages and better conditions.

"Bad news for all bagel fans," wrote the Times. The article also informed the reader that in New York City alone 1,200,000 bagels were consumed each weekend. No wonder that the strike threat had caused panic in the city! The problem was solved, by the way, by an experienced arbitrator and the bagel crisis never took place.

The boom began in New York, but the city was slowly becoming too small for the pioneers of the bagel business. They began to look West for new challenges. Towards the end of the Fifties several bagel bakers decided to set up bakeries in other parts of the country.

One of those who dared to take the step still remembers with amusement how his landlord in Washington DC asked him with incredulity: "And you can really sell these things for seven cents each?" They could – and how! Nowadays many bagel shops are open twenty-four hours a day to supply the demand. In Los Angeles, where nobody walks anywhere, "drive-in" bagel shops have even been set up in the last few years.

The advance of the bagel from the cities of the East Coast to the heart of America wouldn't have been possible, however, without the discovery that bagels are excellent for freezing. In 1962 "Lender's Bagel Bakery" brought the first deep-frozen bagels onto the market. From then on Lender's refrigerated trucks rolled from Connecticut to the farthest corners of the land.

Deep-frozen bagels conquered the supermarkets. For Lender's the discovery was worth its weight in gold: today the company is the largest producer of bagels in America. With 300 employees it produces 12,000 bagels an hour, round the clock.

In the New York Times in 1969 an experienced journalist in the grocery industry wrote in amazement about the new star among the cakes and pastries: "The bagel business isn't what it used to be. It's booming!"

Towards the end of the Seventies the bagel mania spread from America back to Europe. The first bagel bakery was opened in London in August 1977. This event was even reported in the New York Times under the headline: "The American ring rolled as far as London and holed up in Edgewater Street." The Times' London correspondent reported the sensational success of the business to his readers back home – many of them munching on a breakfast of bagels while reading the article. The owner was quoted as follows: "Nobody has asked for their money back. Only one obviously drunken Englishman wanted to exchange his bagels. He wasn't satisfied because he had thought that there was a filling inside."

For more than twenty years the ring has been successfully rolling through Europe, just like hamburgers and hot dogs many years ago.

In England, France and Germany bagels are thought to be typically American – their roots in the Jewish ghettos of Eastern Europe have been long forgotten. When neon signs eventually advertise "hot bagels" in cities such as Warsaw, Cracow or St Petersburg the rings will have finally returned to those places, from which they once set out to conquer the New World.

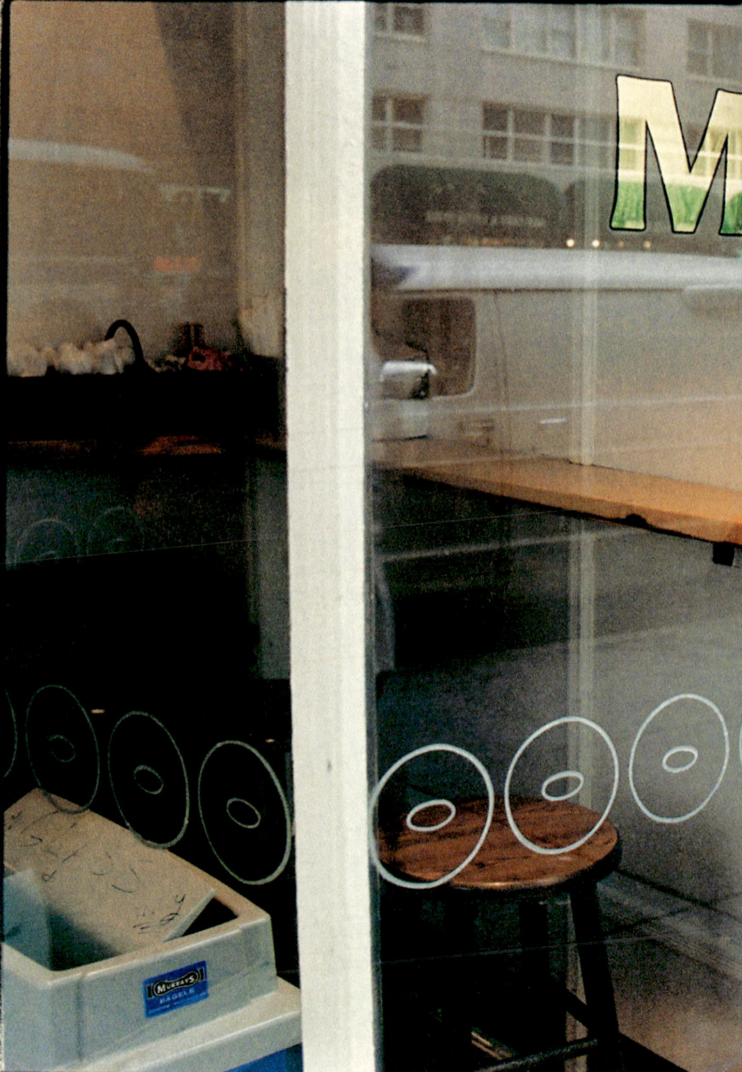
MURRAYS
BAGELS

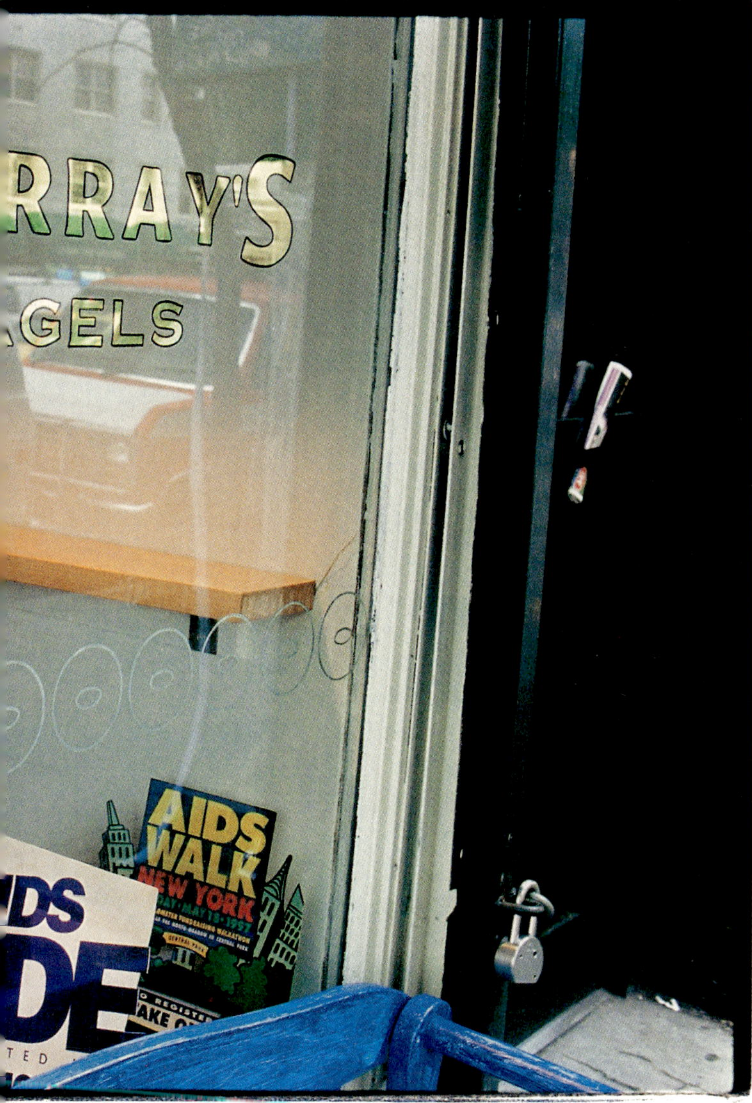
RRAY'S
GELS
AIDS
WALK
NEW YORK

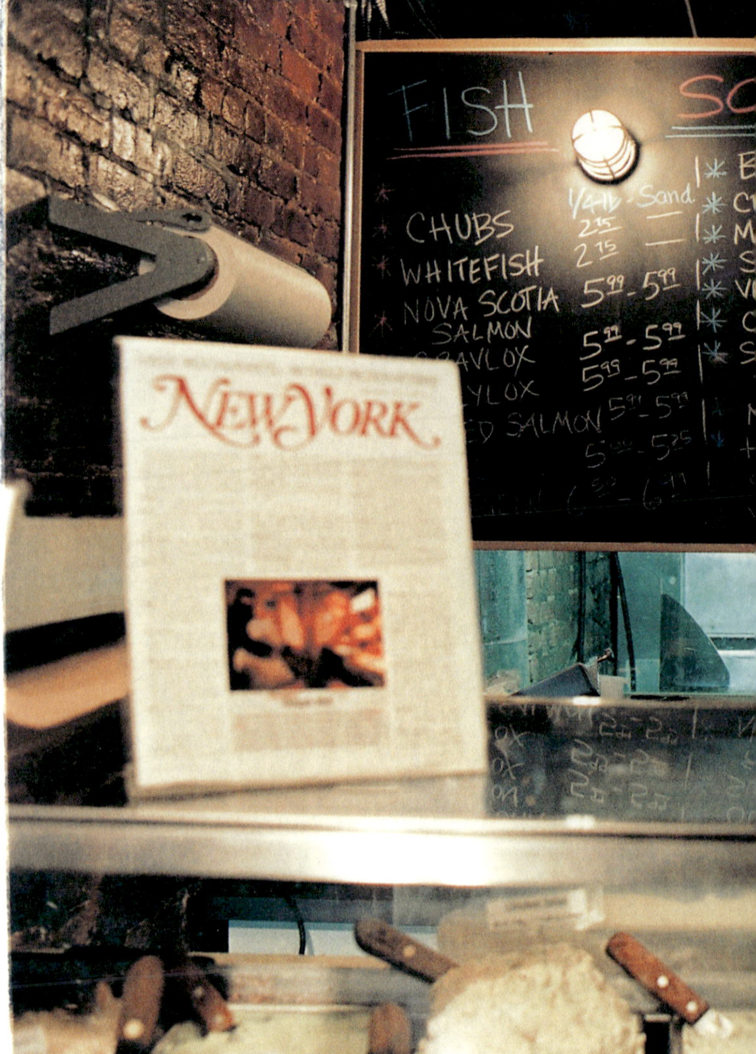

FISH
1/4 lb - Sand
CHUBS 2 15
WHITEFISH 2 15
NOVA SCOTIA SALMON 5 99 - 5 99
NEW YORK

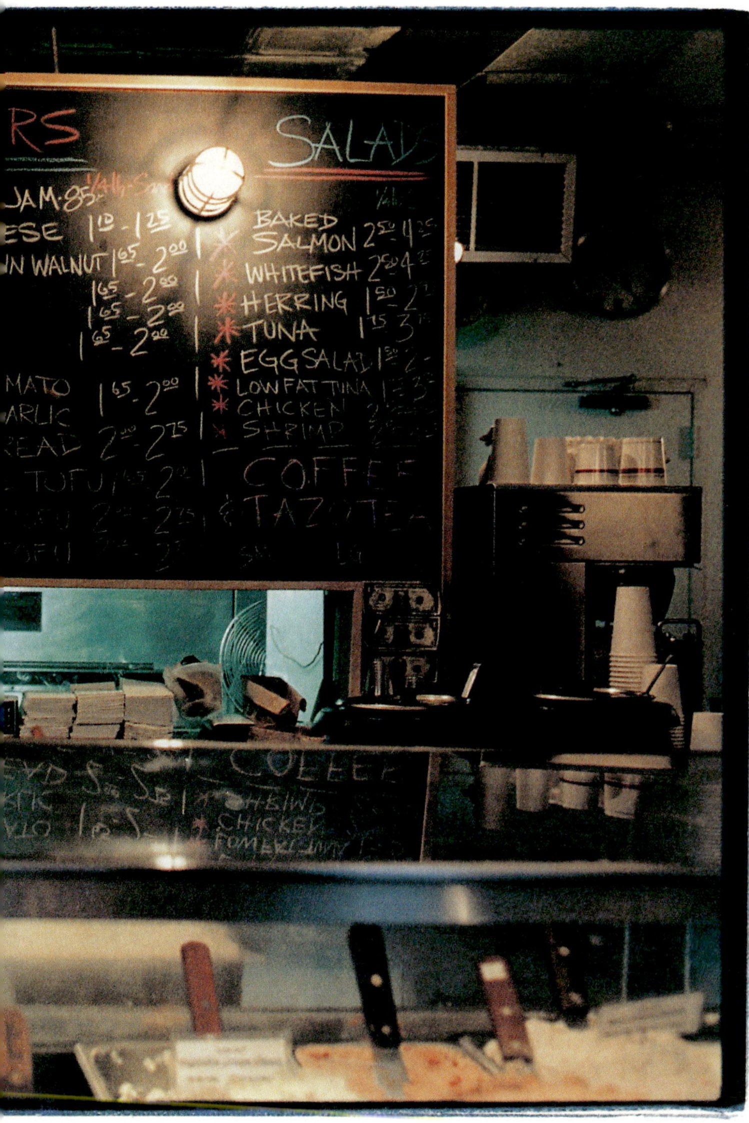

RS
SALADS
BAKED
SALMON
WHITEFISH
HERRING
TUNA
EGG SALAD
LOW FAT TUNA
CHICKEN
SHRIMP
COFFEE
& TAZO TEA
IN WALNUT 1.65 - 2.00

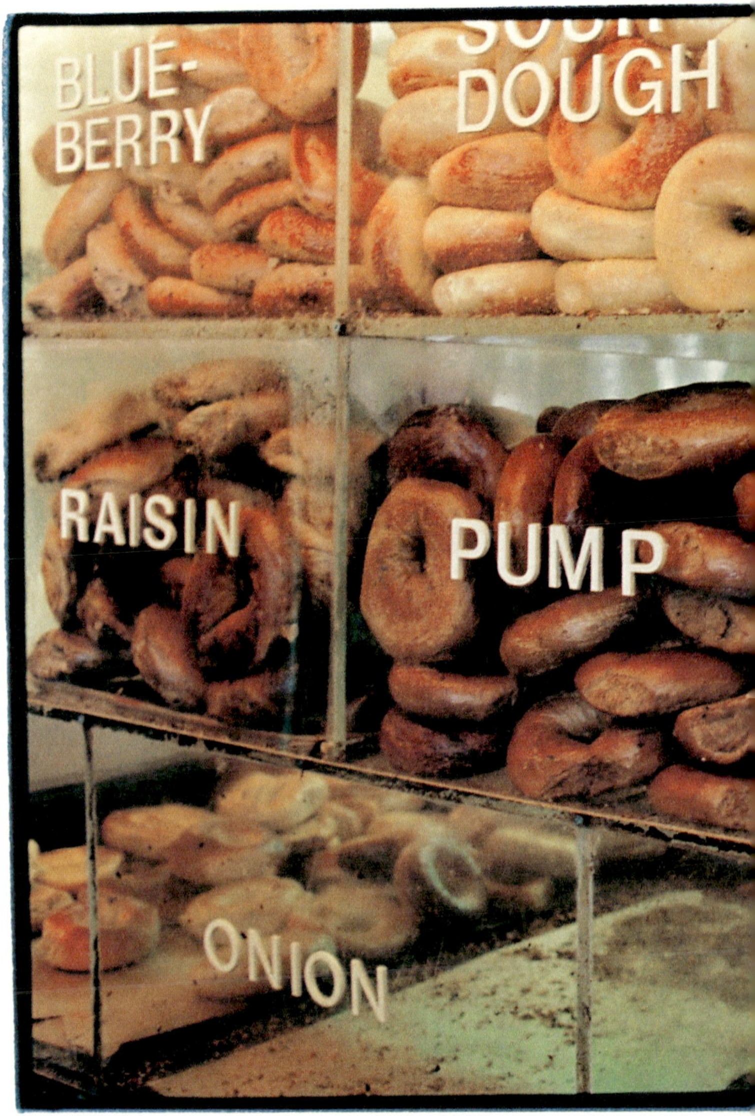

BLUE-
BERRY
DOUGH
RAISIN
PUMP
ONION

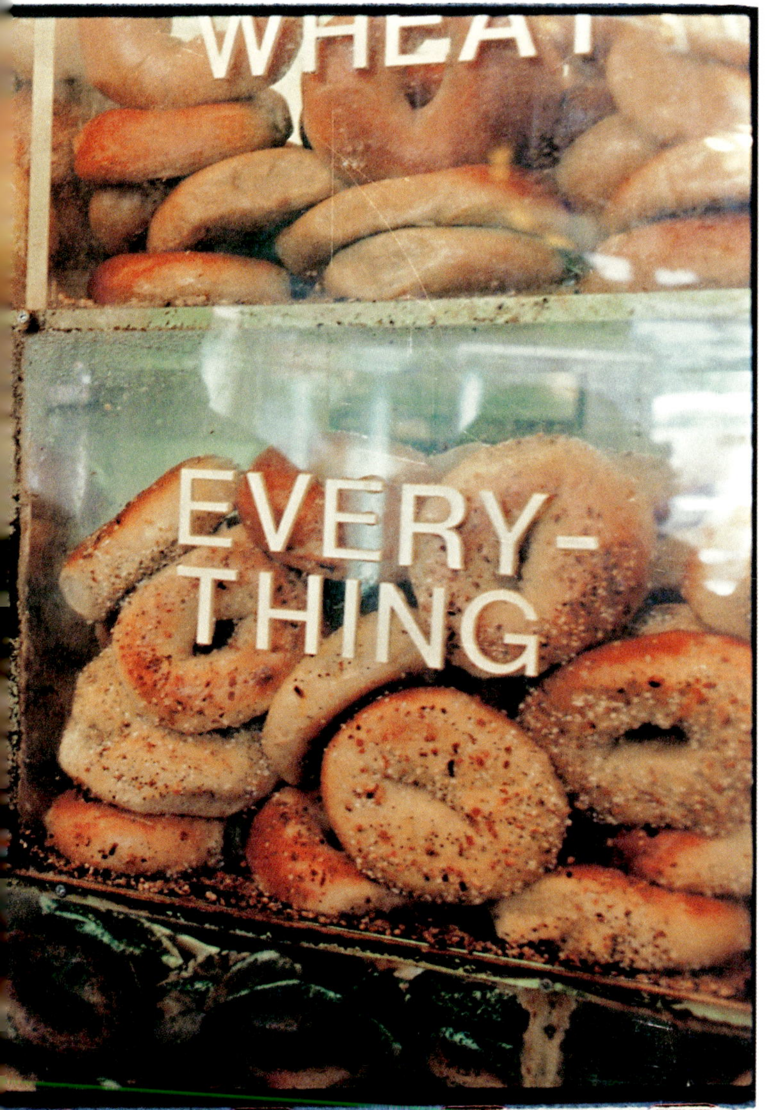
WHEAT
EVERY-
THING

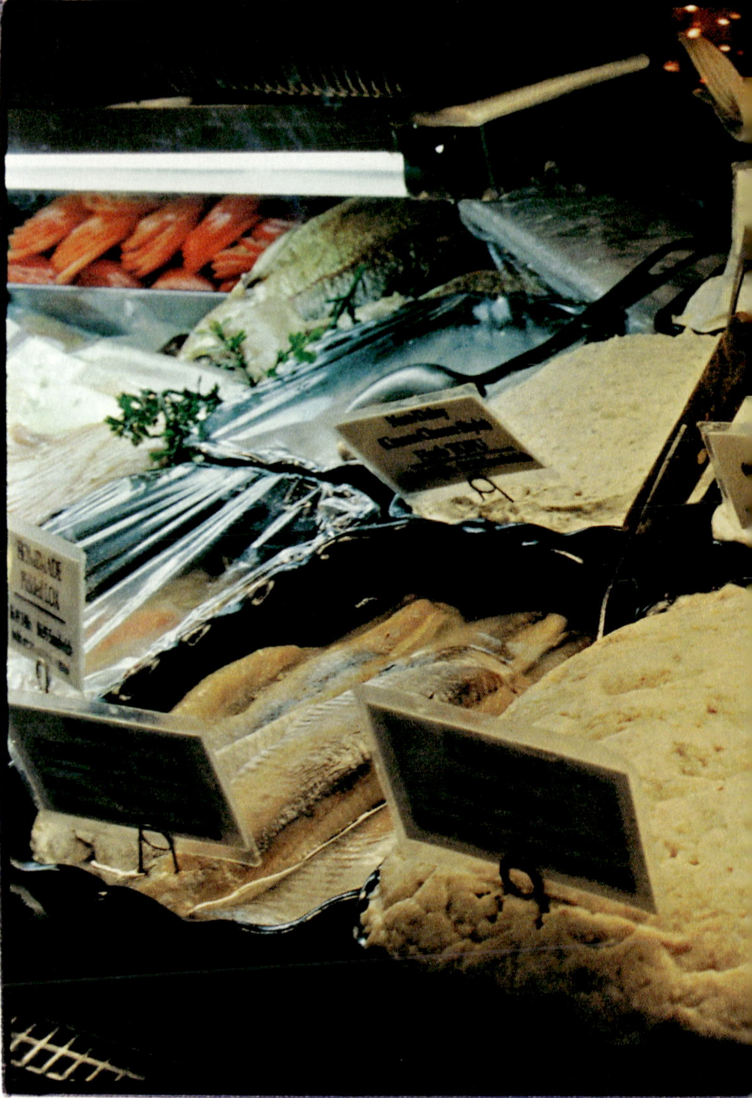

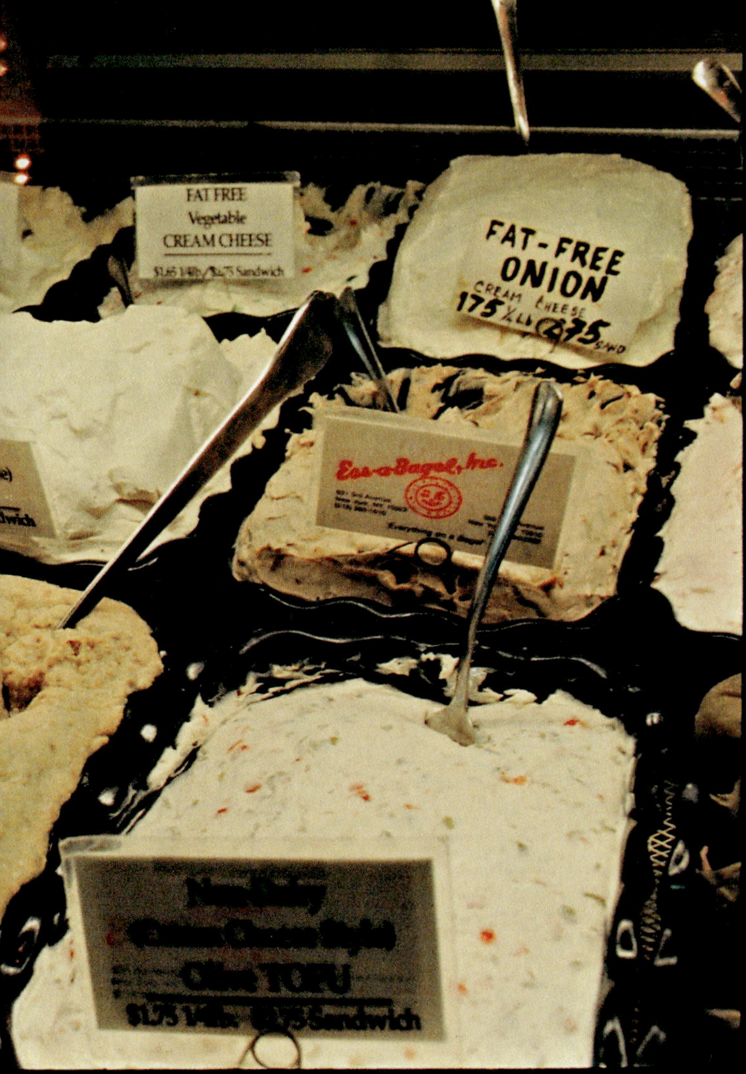
FAT FREE
Vegetable
CREAM CHEESE
FAT-FREE
ONION
CREAM CHEESE
Ess-a-Bagel, Inc.

Bagels

one hole and thousands of possibilities

Bagels are a genuine natural product: flour, yeast, milk, butter, water, a pinch of salt and a single spoon of sugar – these few ingredients, and the necessary baker's know-how, are sufficient to produce the fantastic ring. All bagel bakers use these basic ingredients, although the individual mixture used by the giants in the business is kept strictly secret. The descendants of the immigrant Eastern European bagel bakers established their family fortunes on these valuable basic recipes. That's why they are now safely deposited in the strongboxes of the large bagel dynasties.

In spite of the same basic ingredients there are inumerable variations. One simple alternative is to add eggs to the dough. The bagels are then no longer completely cholesterol-free, which is an important aspect, at least in the United States. However there are further variations: they can be made with different sorts of flour – there are rye bagels, wholemeal bagels, pumpernickel bagels … with poppy, sesame or sunflower seeds or covered in coarse-grained salt. Substantial bagels are given additional flavour with onions, garlic or herbs. For those with a sweet tooth there are cinnamon-raisin bagels. The palette of possibilities still hasn't been exhausted, for the finished bagel itself offers plenty of other opportunities. For example, it can be toasted, grilled, cut into wafer-thin slices then salted or roasted to crisps in the oven.

Bagels are most often eaten with "a shmear", the Yiddish code-word for "cream cheese". The next level are "shmears" with different flavours, fillings, garnishes and sauces that can transform the simple bagel into a highly individual work of art. The classic in this category is still the "bagel with cream cheese and lox". It became extremely fashionable in the Fifties. It first made its début at lavish Sunday brunches in New York and other cities, and was the culinary symbol of American economic achievement. This dish on the table was a proud demonstration: "Look what I can afford." In the meantime bagels with smoked salmon and cream cheese have become rather ordinary.

Nowadays one boasts with French pâté de foie gras or caviar. Other popular variations are fillings of tuna or chicken salad. Some people like to stick herrings between the two halves of the ring. Meat-eaters cover them with roast beef, meat balls or cold cuts; vegetarians prefer raw salads or vegetable fillings.

In addition the bread ring has one further invaluable advantage: it is healthy, cholesterol-free, contains virtually no fat and 1 ¼ oz (37 g) of valuable carbohydrates. An average bagel comes to about 190 calories. For health-food freaks these are telling arguments. However, cholesterol-conscious bagel-fans usually overlook one thing: virtually nobody eats bagels on their own. They are mostly used as a solid basis for thousands of fillings, which for the most part, as far as cholesterol is concerned, are usually pretty considerable.

Apart from individual preferences for different fillings, most people appreciate one quality in particular: bagels don't go soft. The sumptuous filling might squeeze out the sides but the bagel itself never loses its form. It is this very quality that make bagels the only bread that you can eat in bed without regret. There are no annoying crumbs to disturb your sleep, which should be particularly good after enjoying a pleasantly filling bagel.

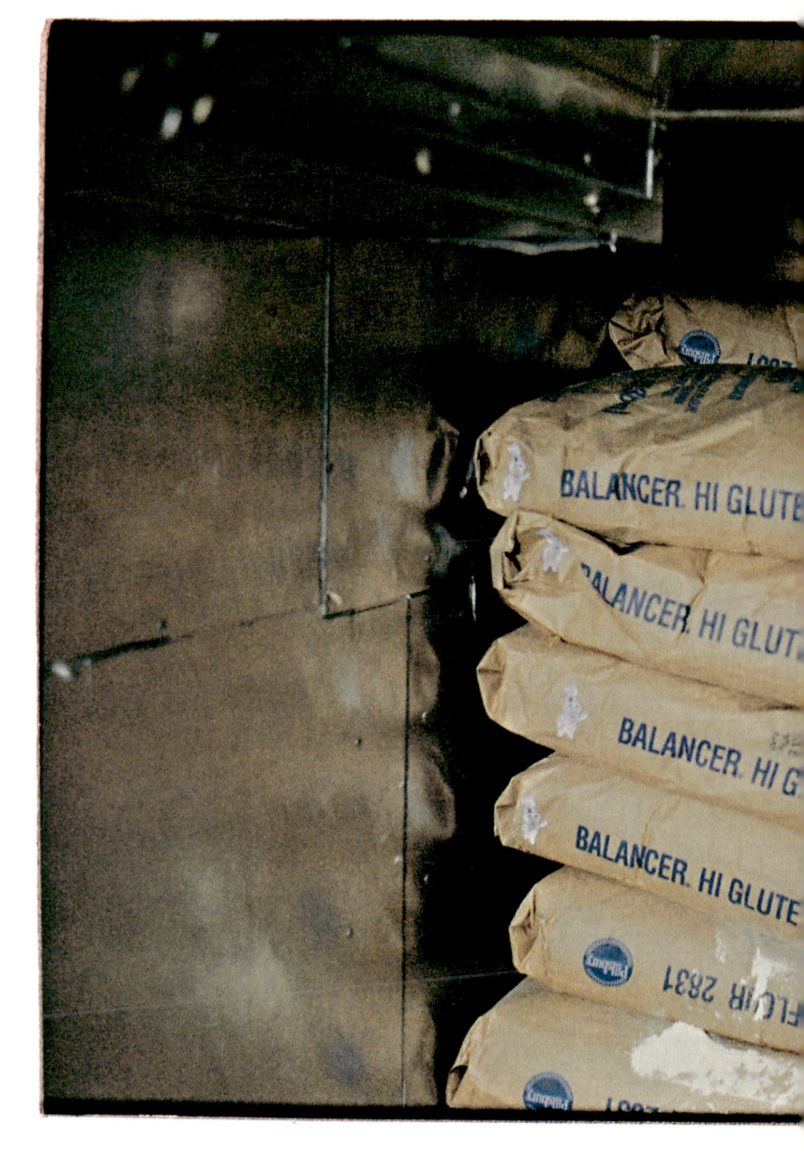
BALANCER. HI GLUTE
BALANCER. HI GLUT
BALANCER. HI G
BALANCER. HI GLUTE
FLOUR 2831

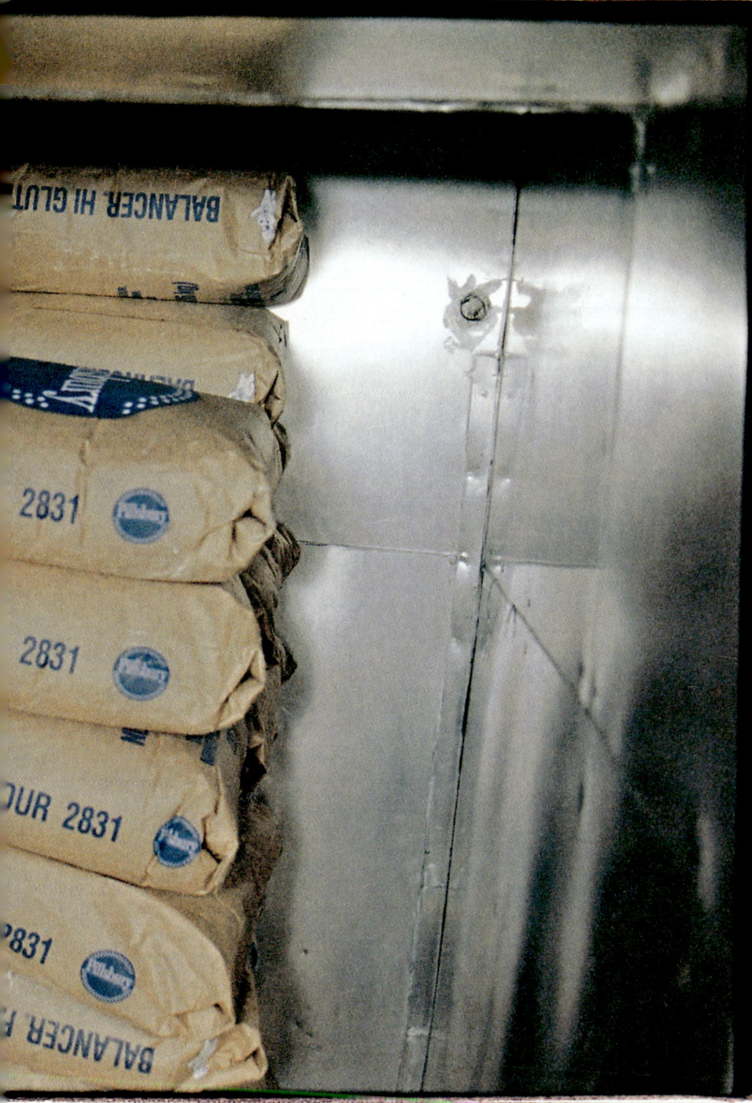
BALANCER HI GLUT
2831
2831
OUR 2831
BALANCER

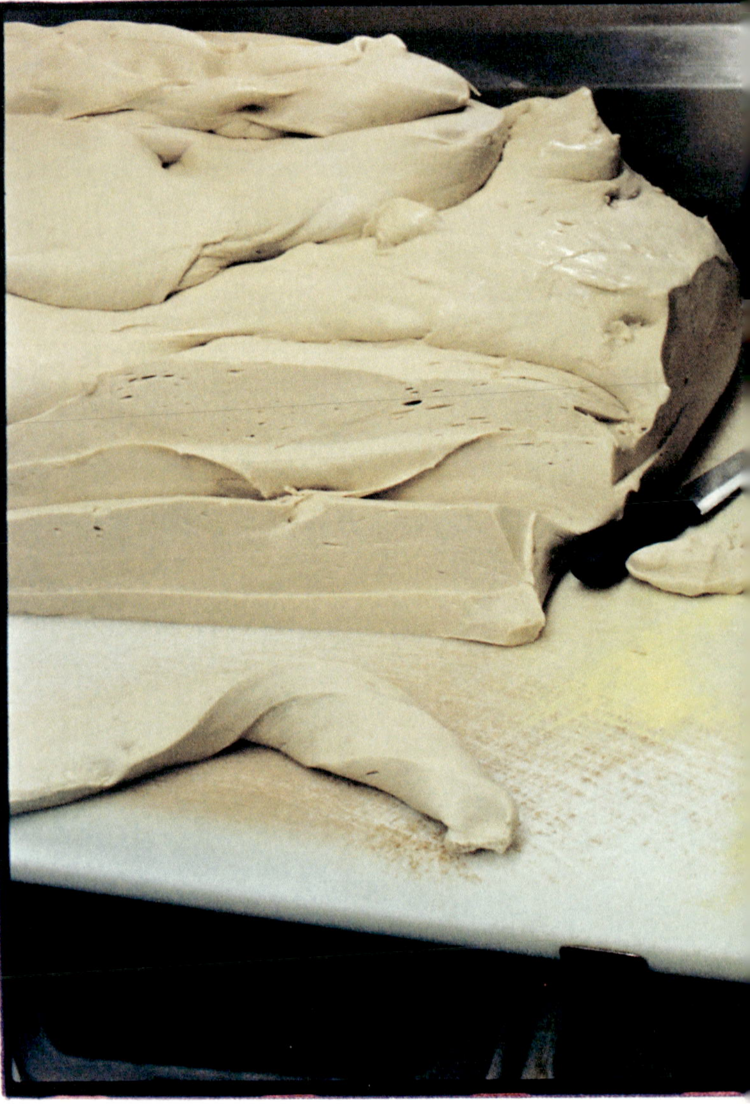

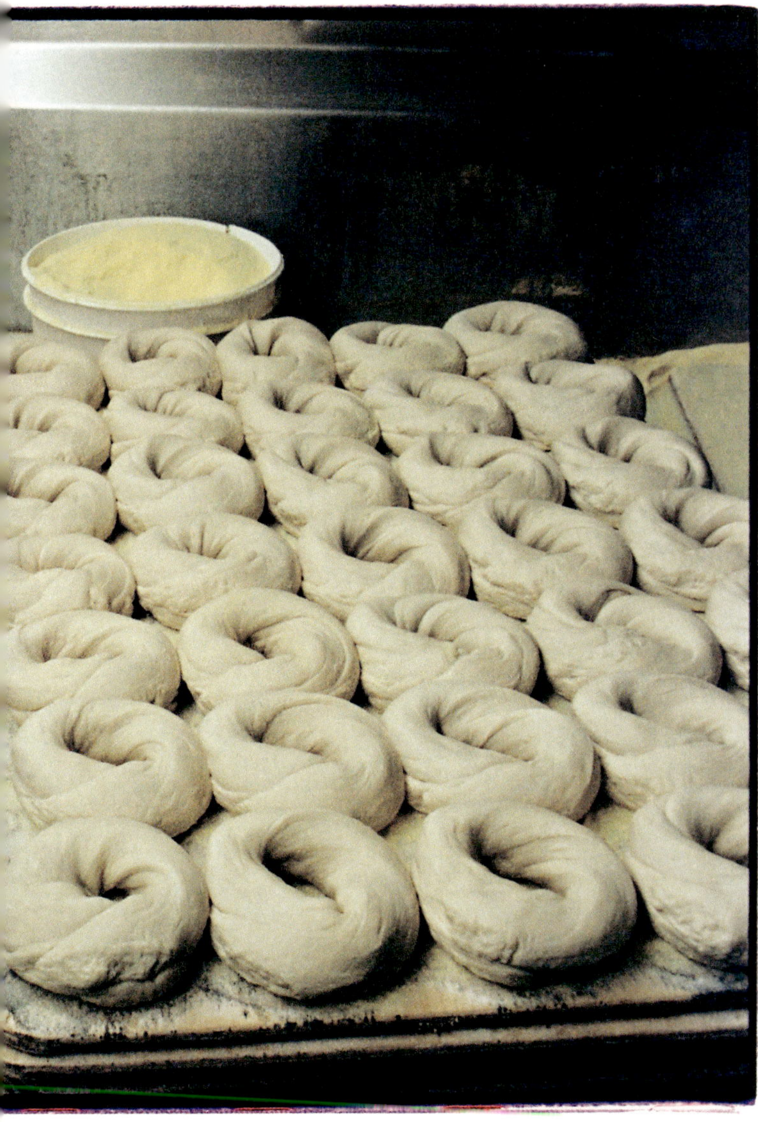

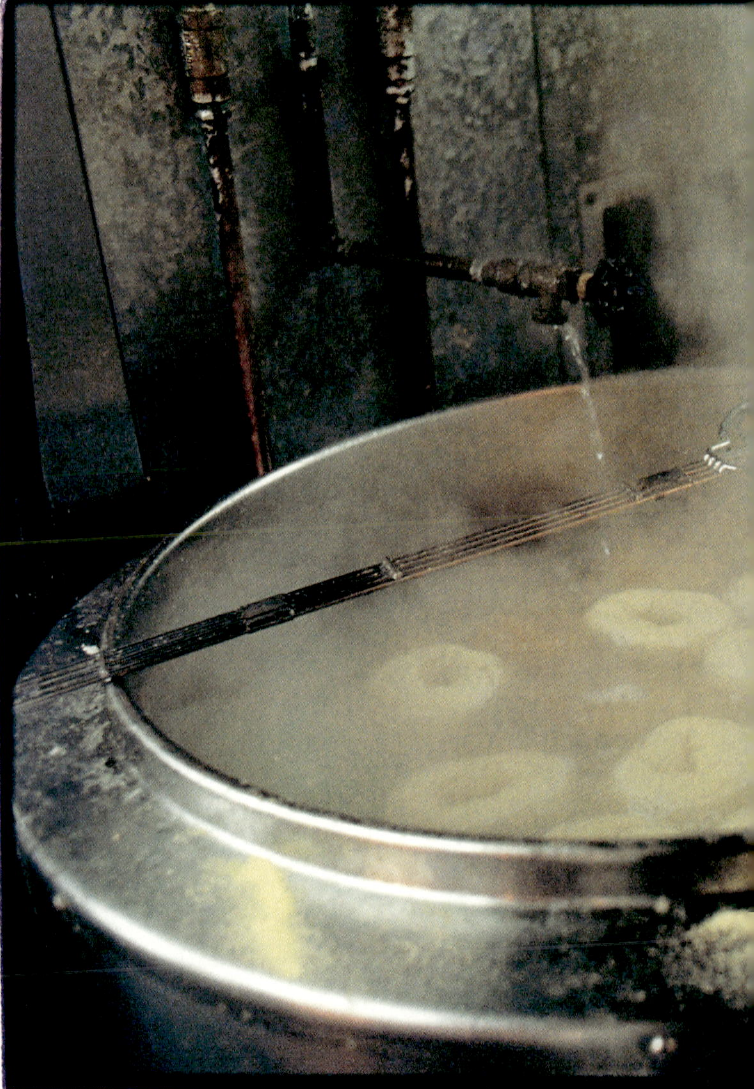

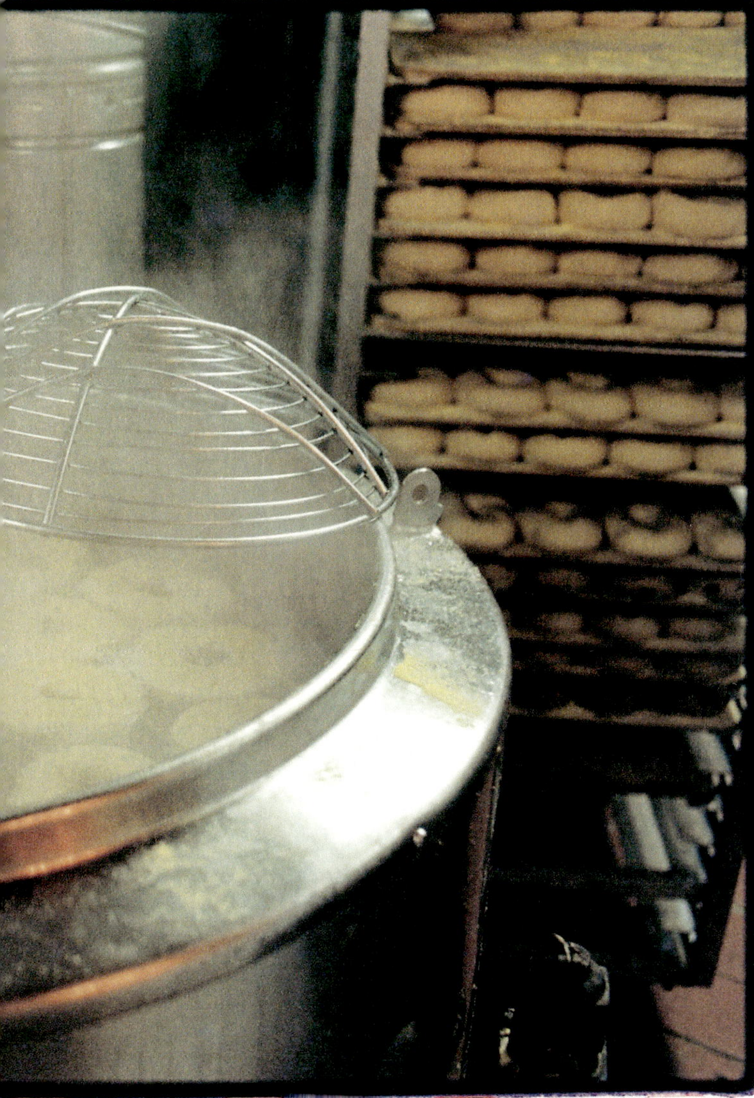

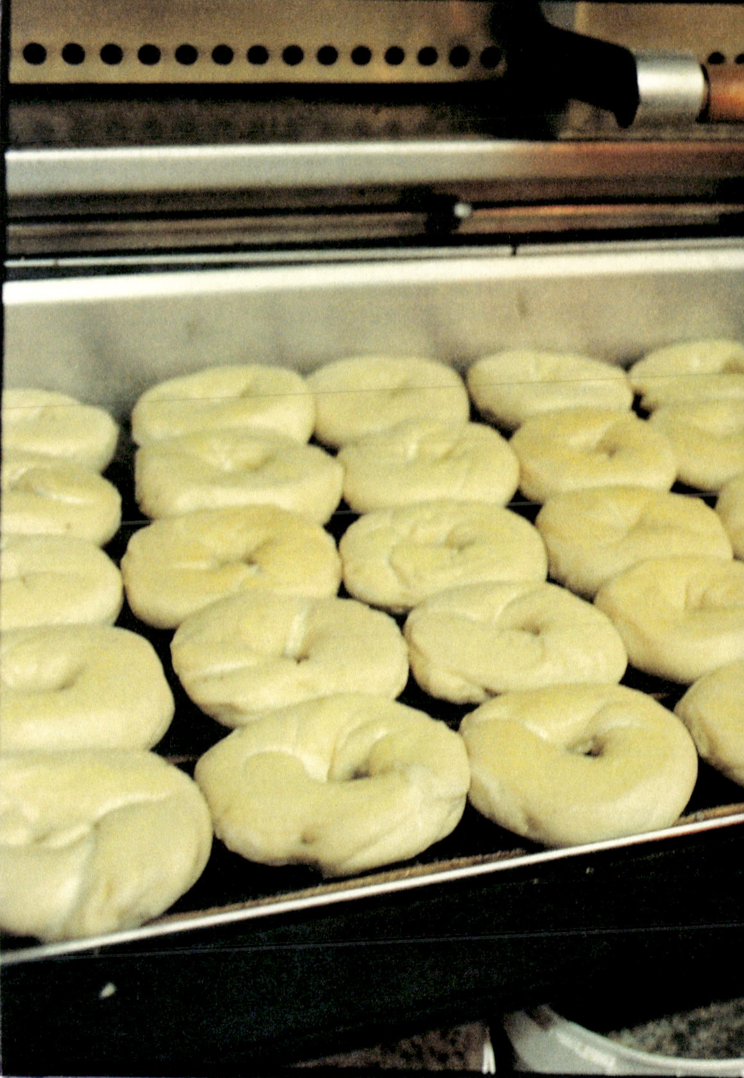

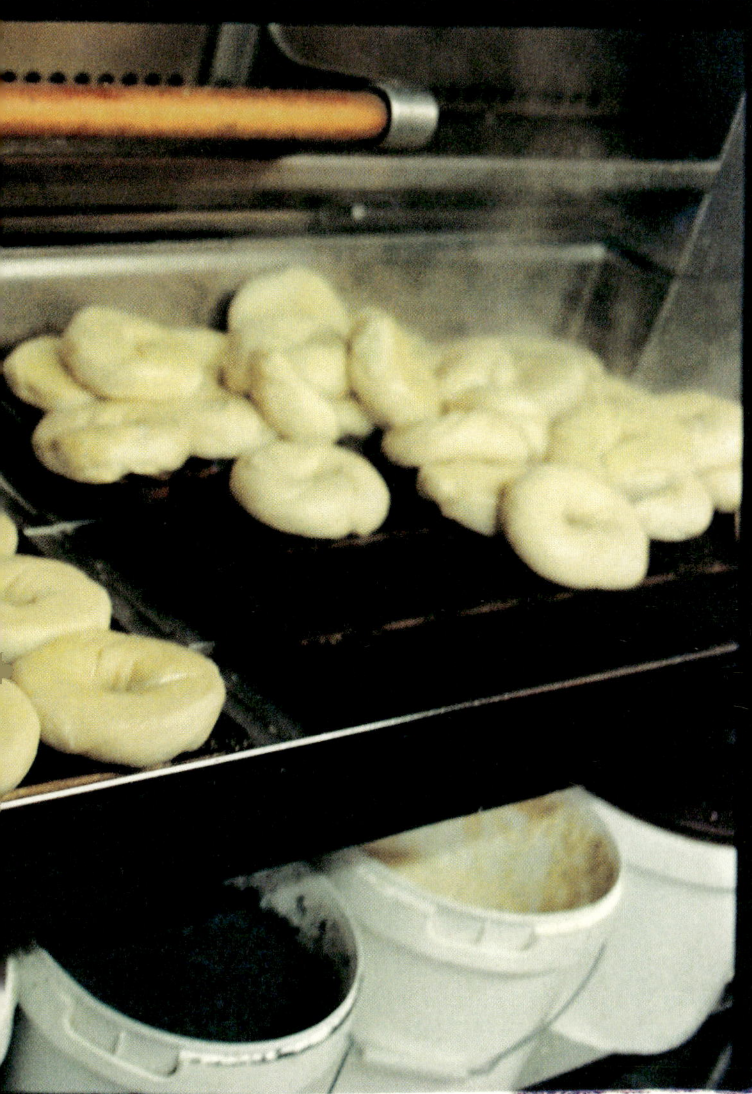

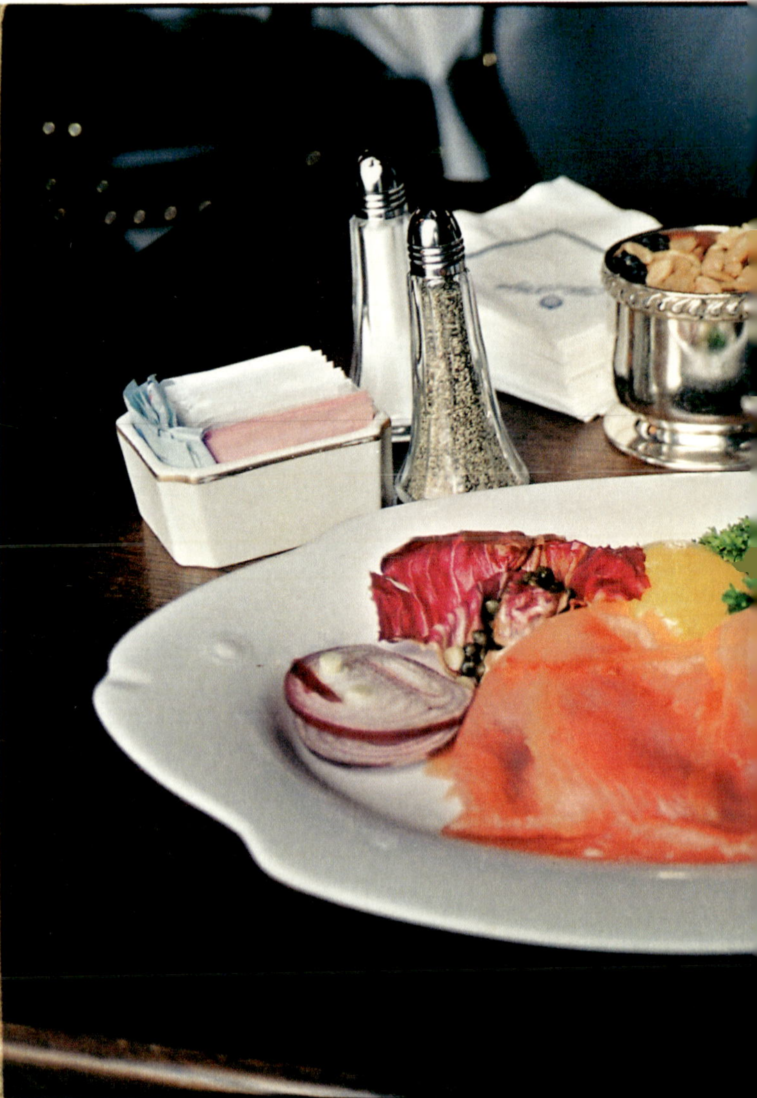

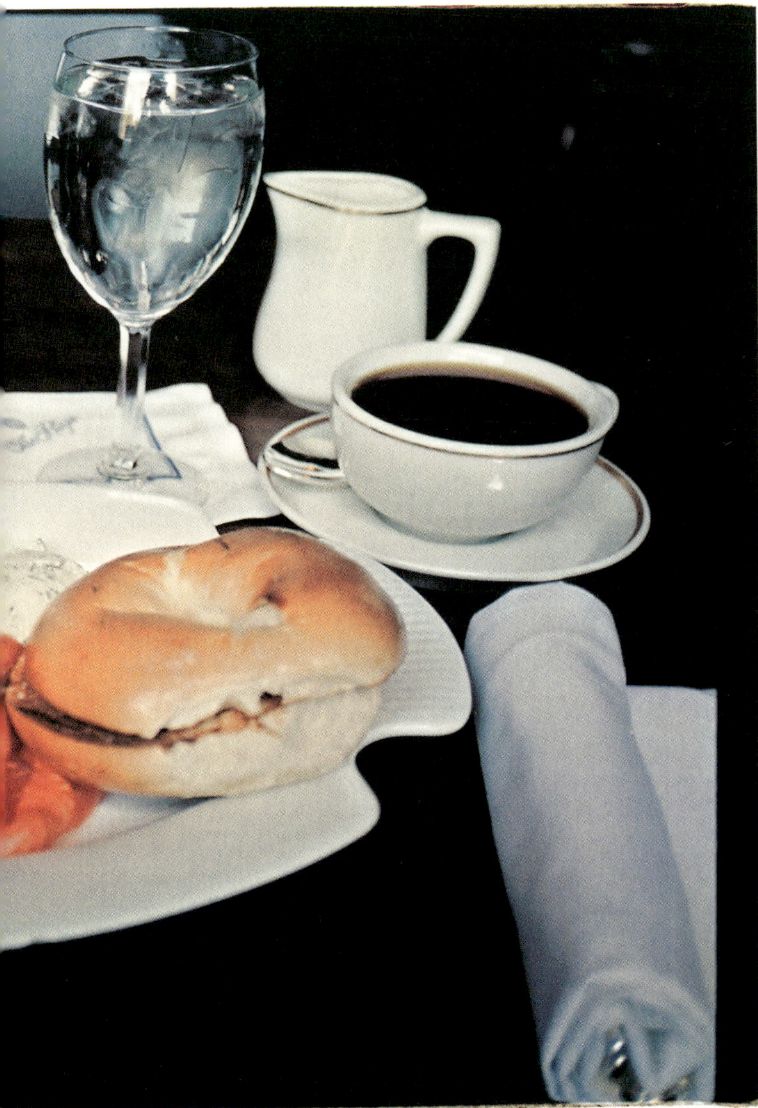

A basic bagel recipe

- 1 cube fresh yeast (approx. 1 oz)
- 1 ½ cups lukewarm water
- 3 tablespoons sugar
- 1 teaspoon salt
- 4 ½ cups sifted, all-purpose flour
- cornflour

Bagel bakers in America use gluten flour for a thicker consistency. Gluten is available in America, but it can also be replaced with cornflour. Either 1 oz (25 g) gluten or 2 oz (50 g) edible starch is mixed thoroughly into the flour.

1. Put half of the flour into a large mixing bowl, forming a depression in the middle. Dissolve the yeast in ½ cup of lukewarm water, add sugar and pour the mixture into the depression. Sprinkle lightly with flour. Let the yeast rise, until the surface flour is cracked.

2. Add the remaining cup of lukewarm water and the salt. Mix together and knead in the remaining flour until the dough is smooth. Cover the dough with a cloth and leave in a warm place for approx. 30 minutes to rise.

3. Once the dough has risen knead it again on a surface covered with flour and divide into 8–10 portions. Roll these into sausages, wrap around a finger, dampen the ends and press together. Put the bagels on a baking tray covered with flour and leave to stand for 20 minutes.

4. Boil 6 pints (3 l) of water in a large pan. Reduce the heat and put 3–4 bagels in the simmering water. Leave in uncovered pan for 7 minutes (not longer!). Take out of the pan with a slotted spoon and leave to dry on a cloth. Repeat procedure for the other bagels.

5. Preheat the oven to gas mark 6, 400 °F (200 °C) and bake the bagels for 40–50 minutes. Allow to cool on a wire tray.

Variation:
To cover the bagels with poppy, sesame or sunflower seeds, whisk 1 egg-white with 1 tablespoon water. Take the baking tray with the bagels out of the oven after approx. 10 minutes, coat them with the egg-white mixture and sprinkle with the seeds then continue baking.

Bagels are mostly served with "a shmear". The simplest variation is cream cheese on its own. This can however either be mixed with fresh herbs and onions or it can serve as a spreadable basis for anything you like that can be mixed into cream cheese: tuna, chicken, dried or fresh tomatoes, avocado and other vegetables.

The "classic" version is cream cheese with smoked salmon and onion rings. However there are no limits to your own initiative and fantasy: "freestyle" is the name of the game! For example: a layer of thin slices of tomatoes and mozzarella, with pesto sauce or salami, on thinly-buttered bagel halves … and the "bagel italienne" is ready!

If you wish to eat according to kosher requirements, however, you must be careful not to combine meat and dairy products, and get the ingredients in kosher foodstores.

Waldorf chicken filling

- 1 ½ cups cooked chicken
- 1 spring onion, with the green finely chopped
- 1 apple, cored, peeled and sliced
- 1 stick celery, finely chopped
- ¼ cup of raisins
- ¼ cup almond slices
- ¼ cup mayonnaise
- 1 teaspoon lemon juice
- ½ teaspoon salt
- ½ teaspoon sugar
- pinch of pepper
- a few salad leaves
- 1 small carrot, roughly grated
- 2 bagels

1. Mix together ingredients from chicken to almond slices.

2. Whisk the mayonnaise, lemon juice, salt and sugar to a sauce and pour over the meat mixture.

3. Divide the salad leaves on four bagel halves. Spread the mixture on the salad leaves and garnish with the grated carrot.

Bagels with "a bit of everything"

- ½ cup mayonnaise
- 1 teaspoon German mustard
- 1 tablespoon finely chopped onion
- ½ teaspoon celery seeds
- 1 medium-sized pickled gherkin, finely chopped
- 1 pinch pepper
- 2 cups finely chopped white cabbage
- 4 slices mature Dutch cheese or 4 oz (100 g) sliced corned beef and 4 slices liver sausage
- 4 pickled gherkins, sliced lengthways
- 4 radishes, cut into roses
- 2 bagels

1. Mix the mayonnaise, mustard, onions, gherkin, celery seeds and pepper into a sauce. Mix with the chopped white cabbage in a small bowl. Leave uncovered in the refrigerator to marinate.

2. Spread half the cabbage salad on the bagels halves and cover with either the slices of corned beef or the cheese. Spread the rest of the cabbage salad on top and cover the corned beef version with the liver sausage.

3. Garnish with two gherkin halves and a radish skewered on a tooth pick.

Bagels with chicken liver

- 1 ½ lb (700 g) chicken liver
- ½ tablespoon vegetable oil
- ¼ cup margarine
- 2 medium-sized onions, finely chopped
- 4 hard-boiled eggs, chopped
- 2 teaspoons salt
- 4 (onion) bagels
- radish slices

1. Brown the chicken liver quickly. Then place it in a pan and cover with water. Boil the water then reduce the heat and simmer on a small flame (without the lid) for approx. 1 ½ hours.

2. Heat the oil and the margarine in a large pan. Fry the onions until they are soft. Remove the pan from the heat. Add the chicken liver and eggs to the onions. Mash the liver with a fork and mix everything together into a rough mixture. Leave the mixture to cool (uncovered) in the refrigerator.

3. Spread the bagel halves thickly with the liver mixture and garnish with the slices of radish.

Bagels with gefilte fish

- 3 tablespoons chopped onions
- 10 oz (250 g) beetroot (from a jar), dried and finely chopped
- 2 tablespoons vinegar
- ½ teaspoon sugar
- a pinch of pepper
- 4 oz (100 g) cream cheese
- 1 ⅓ tablespoons horseradish (from a jar)
- 4 pieces gefilte fish*, cut into slices
- 1 spring onion, with the green finely chopped
- 1 carrot, sliced lengthways
- 4 bagels

* gefilte fish is available in kosher foodstores

1. Mix all the ingredients from the onions to the pepper. Leave to marinate in a cool place for a few hours.

2. Mix the cream cheese with the horseradish and spread on the bagels. Cover the bagels with the beetroot mixture. Lay the slices of gefilte fish on top. Garnish with the chopped spring onion and carrot slices.

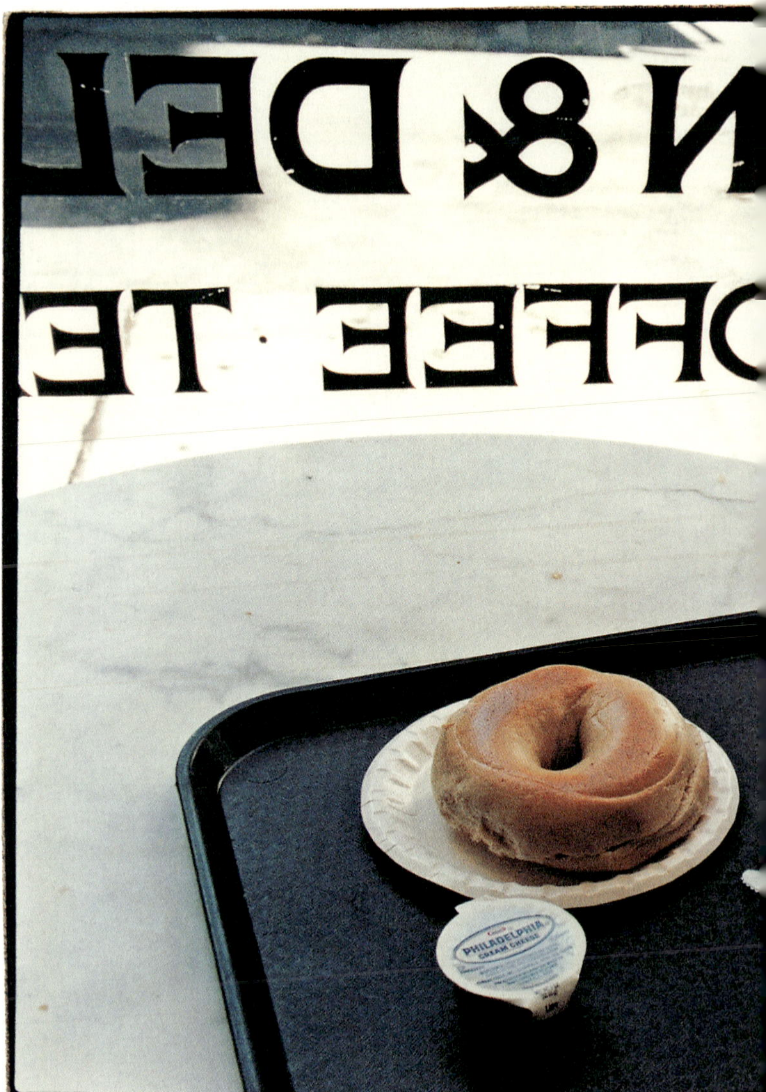

PHILADELPHIA
CREAM CHEESE

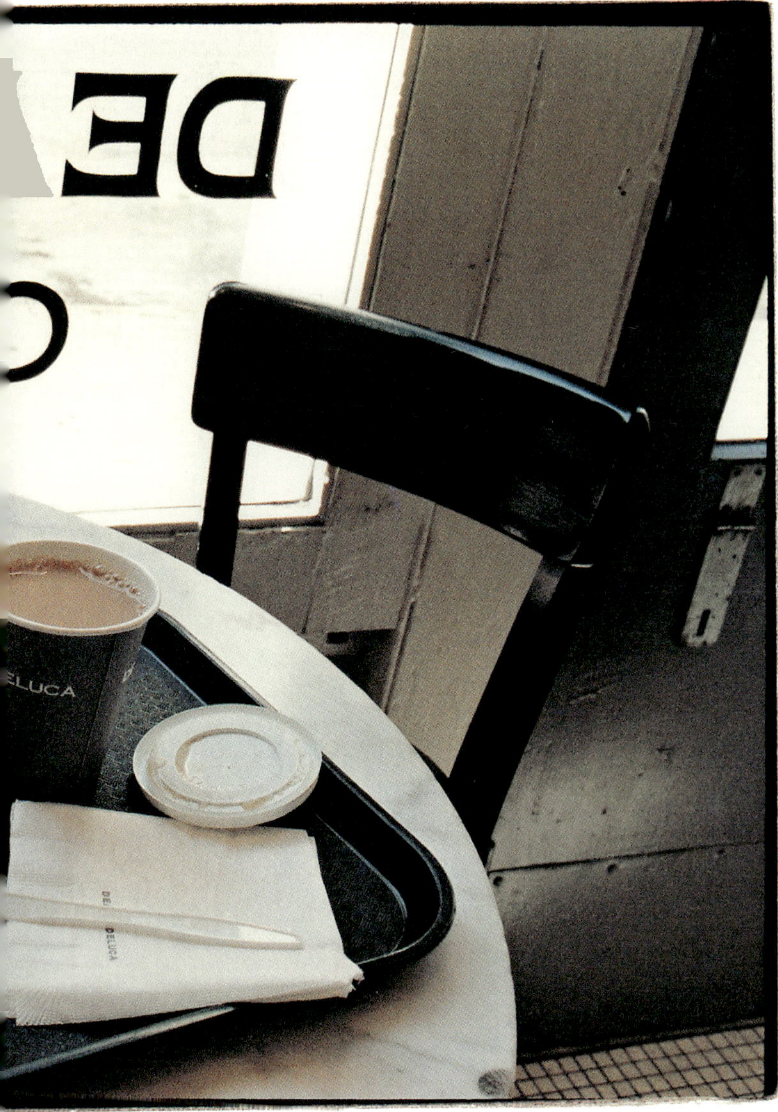
ELUCA
DE
DELUCA

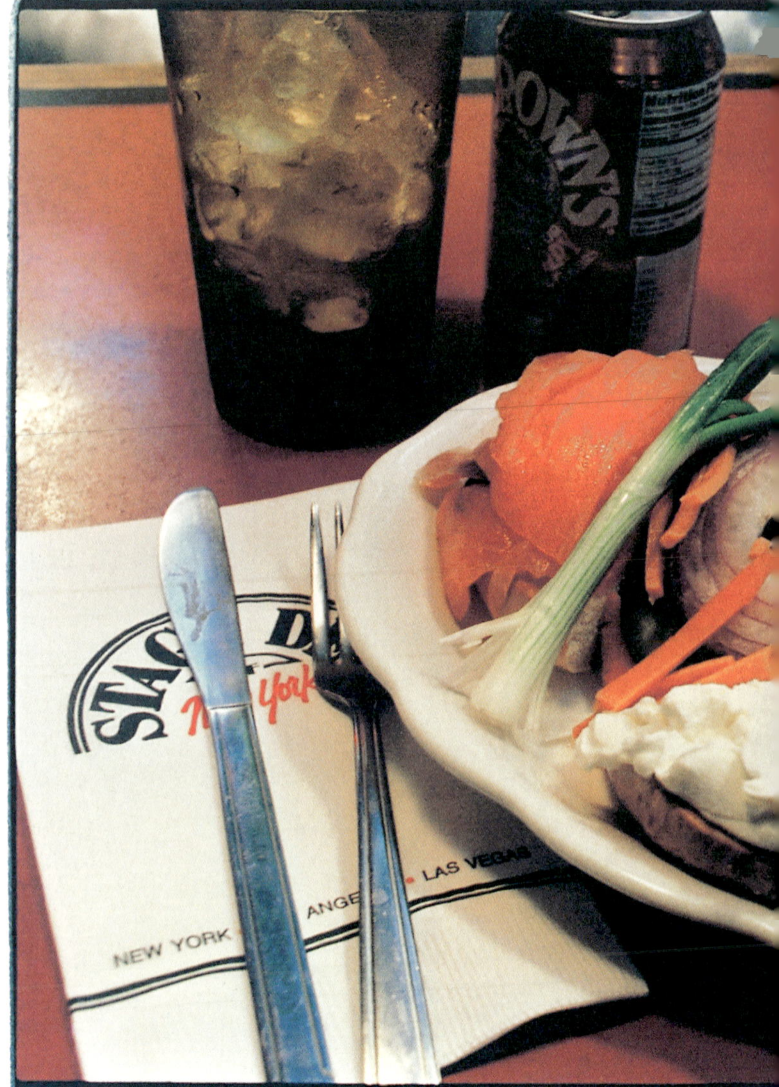

NEW YORK
LAS VEGAS

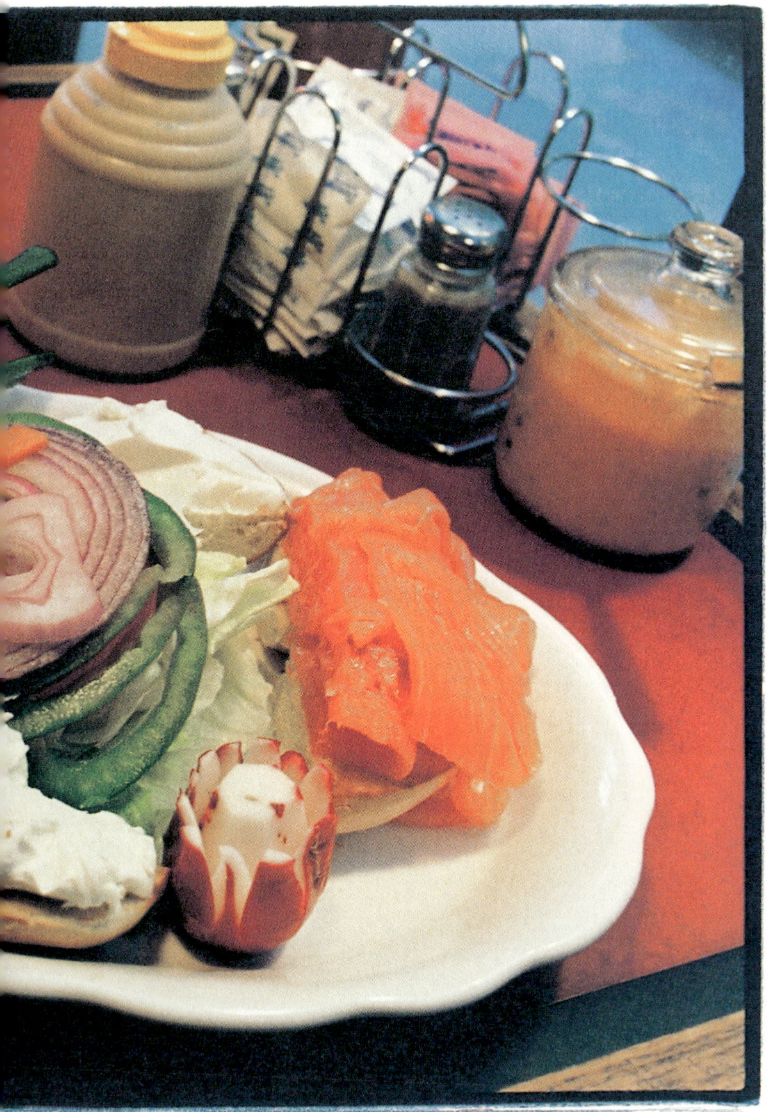

Bagels on the Internet
by Rudi Konar

Is there more to the bagel than meets the eye? What is the real truth behind the bagel? Where will it all lead?

If you are alone in your kitchen discussing this and other questions with your bagel, there is help at hand: you are not alone. Somewhere out there are other devoted fans, bagel afficionados, bagel experts, bagel professionals, bagel addicts or just plain simple bagel eaters. As "bagelites" can now be found spread right across the globe, they communicate in the one medium where geography is not important: the Internet. There are any number of Internet adresses dedicated solely to the bagel. Some are just small bagel shops, like **www.whatsabagel.com** or **www.tastybagel.com**, that want to whet your appetite, others such as the Bagel Oasis (**www.bageloasis.com**) provide a mail-order bagel service. Unfortunately for Europeans, the handmade oven-ready bagels are only delivered in the USA.

Bagels are big business: once you have acquired the taste, you can easily turn your passion into a career – surf over to the Bagel Consulting Services (**www.bagels.net**) and buy a second-hand bagel restaurant for $70,000, including décor and toaster. It's easy to change from junkie to dealer. Or you can take out a franchise on your own bagel temple. Manhattan Bagel calculates that with $150,000 you can open your own restaurant, including the cost of the great opening party and the uniforms for the staff (**www.manhattanbagel.com**).

Bagels are not of this world: on the Internet you can find the proof that bagels have very special origins. At **www.bagelnet.com/pyrmd.html** you can discover that their form is derived from remnants of the early spaceships that were instrumental in building the Egyptian pyramids. It was always unlikely that the heavenly bagel should have been created on earth; now we have the proof.

Bagels cause problems: if you listen in to the discussions of stressed fast-food managers (web newsgroup alt.mcdonalds) you will get to know the darker side of bagel-mania. While one manager is proud to report that "his region has successfully kept the bagel off the menu", a certain George replies that "bagels are a big hit. We even sell 12 boxes a week." It soon becomes clear, however, why the fast-food managers are so scared of the bagel: a bagel requires time and dedication, which even George doesn't have much of. "You soon realize, that the people that developed the bagel don't have any idea what we have to put up with here." Incidentally, George advises that the bagels be pre-cut, in order to save time. Awful. Perhaps with one of those sadistic bagel-guillotines, like the "Bagel Biter", that's on offer at **www.jewishsource.com** for $ 29.95. There you can also purchase the "Acrylic Bagel Holder" ($ 10.95), which is somehow reminiscent of an aquarium, but which is supposed to stop the bagel running away during the obligatory cutting procedure. You can recognize the true fan by his or her "Bagel Breakfast Mug": it looks like a bagel with a handle, the hole is included in the $10.00 price-tag.

Bagels are international: it is immediately apparent on the Internet that the bagel fanclub is spread across the whole world. For example, a Japanese "bagelite" describes his "first time" and you can click on the holiday snaps from Canada at the same time (**www.orange.ne.jp/~kitako/bagel/bagelwh.htm**).

Germany has also been bitten by the bagel bug and thanks to "Bagelbrothers" you can now enjoy your bagels in Leipzig and Essen. Their website is a good tip for first-timers: thanks to revolving 3D-graphics of poppy seed, sesame seed, wholemeal, onion and blueberry bagels, beginners can also see what the delicious ring really looks like (**www.leipzig-kommt.com/bagel**).

Bagels can be tough: and when the going gets tough, the tough get going. For the toughest of the tough there is the "Golden Bagel Award", which the snowboarders and mountainbikers of the Fat Bagel Racing Team award each year (**www.fatbagel.com**). The award categories (e.g. Best Crash of the Year) are a reward for broken ribs and scraped knees.

Bagels are art: there are still traces left on the Internet of the video installation "Bagels", which among other things shows a kosher "Oriental Speciality Snack Bar" for 90 minutes (**www.blinx.de/allgirls**). Four people enter the snack bar during this time. The reason behind these Warhol-like observations dating from 1992 was the reintroduction of the bagel to Berlin.

In the meantime you can also get them without oriental flavours (**www.salomon-bagels.com**).

After this trip through the virtual world you can finally surf over to **www.freeweb.pdq.net/shoe** and chat to other "bagelites" and relate your own experiences. Here you will also find a comprehensive library of bagel stories, for example how a bagel saved the life of Adrienne R. during World War II. Or the true history of the bagel. There is also a shrine for the "hole with a bit of dough around it". And if after all that you still don't feel like biting into a bagel straight away, then nobody can help you.

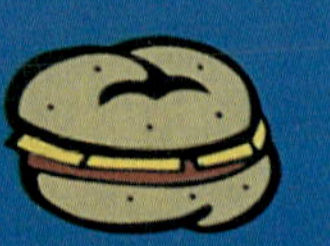
BREAKFAST
HOT
ALL BAKING DONE ON
BOARS HEAD COLD

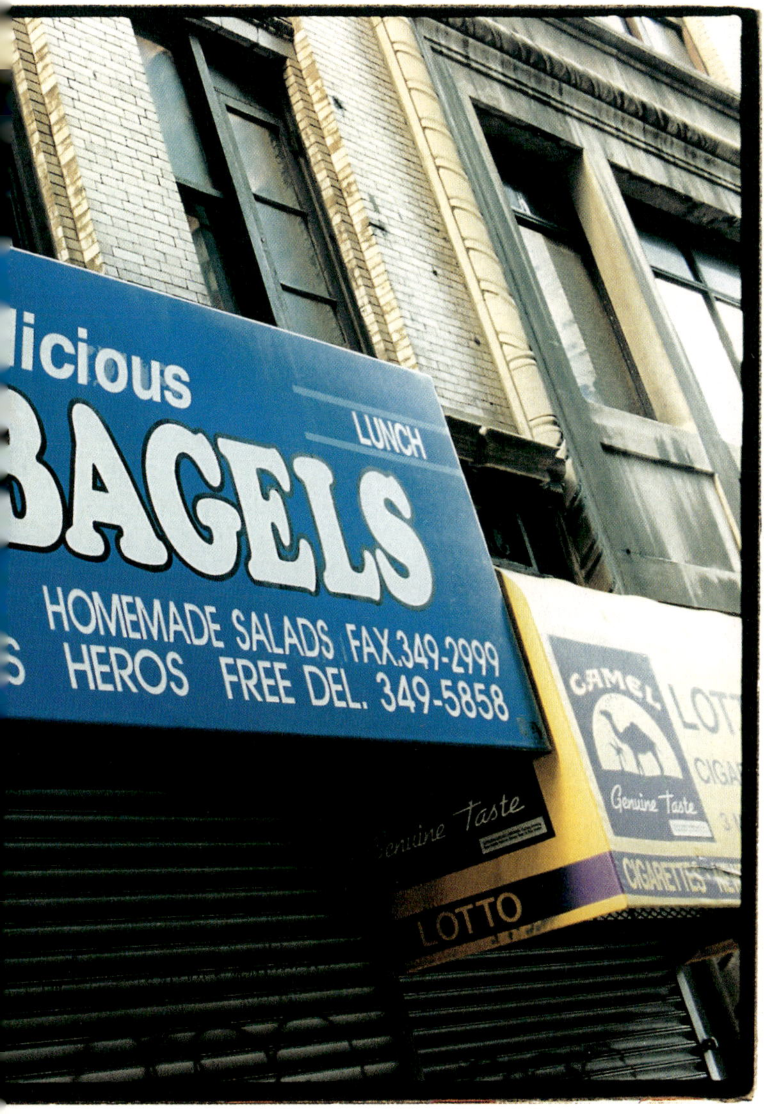

licious
BAGELS
LUNCH
HOMEMADE SALADS FAX.349-2999
S HEROS FREE DEL. 349-5858
Genuine Taste
LOTTO
CAMEL
Genuine Taste
LOTT
CIGA
CIGARETTES

Text by Eric Friedler
Photographs by Peter Loewy
With a text contribution by Rudi Konar

Translated into English by James Abram

Special thanks to Barbara Siebert

Thanks to Ellen Presser and P. J. Blumenthal for the transcription of the bagel song

Gina Kehayoff Verlag
Herzogstrasse 60
D-80803 Munich
Tel. +49 89 39 01 85
Fax +49 89 33 80 53
kehayoff@compuserve.com

Kehayoff books are available worldwide. Please contact your nearest bookseller or write to either of the following addresses for information concerning your local distributor:

Kehayoff c/o Prestel
Mandlstrasse 26
D-80802 Munich
Tel. +49 89 381 70 90
Fax +49 89 381 70 935
sales@prestel.de

and
16 West 22nd Street
New York, NY 10010, USA
Tel. 212 627-8199
Fax 212 627-9866

Layout: Andrés Gomez, H3A, Munich
Printed and bound in Germany

ISBN 3-929078-63-5